THE
ART
OF
CROSSING
CULTURES

THE ART OF CROSSING CULTURES

Craig Storti

INTERCULTURAL PRESS, INC.

For information, contact
Intercultural Press, Inc.
P.O. Box 700
Yarmouth, ME 04096 USA

Library of Congress Catalog No. 89–084387
ISBN 0–933662–85–8

Library of Congress Cataloging-in-Publication Data

Storti, Craig.
    The art of crossing cultures / Craig Storti.
        p.   cm.
    Includes bibliographical references.
    ISBN 0–933662–85–8
    1. Culture shock. 2. Intercultural communication.
    3. Assimilation. I. Title.
    GN517.S76   1989   89–84387
    303.48'2—dc20   CIP

Printed in the United States of America.

To my Teachers,
Mother Sayama
and Saya U Chit Tin,
with deepest respect
and gratitude

Craig Storti, a former Peace Corps volunteer and trainer, has his own intercultural consulting business—Crossing Cultures—and is a partner in The Business Communications Group of Washington, DC. He is the author of *Incident At Bitter Creek* and has had articles published in numerous magazines and newspapers, including Yankee, Signature, The Washington *Post* and The Los Angeles *Times.*

Contents

Foreword

Once every decade in every discipline of study, a book comes along which does more than inform and entertain. It enlightens. I have a hunch that *The Art of Crossing Cultures* will be such a book for the intercultural field.

The interesting thing about *The Art of Crossing Cultures* is that it will be as enlightening to the university student in a formal intercultural communication course as it will be to the practical-minded businessperson bound for a first overseas assignment and as it will be for the seasoned intercultural specialist who is forever looking for theoretical material to explain the process we have all experienced but have such difficulty putting into words.

The selected quotations from literary sources are themselves worth the price of the book. They are truly delightful, making their points with clarity and charm, and adding their own additional insights to those of Craig Storti.

It is a pleasure to discover such a literate new writer contributing to our field and to share, even for a moment, this paper podium with him.

L. ROBERT KOHLS
San Francisco
February 1989

Acknowledgements

I am grateful for this opportunity to acknowledge a number of people who have helped *The Art of Crossing Cultures* see the light of day.

I want first to thank Sandra Fowler, Fanchon Silberstein and Robert Kohls whose generous support and encouragement came at a time when they mattered most.

For their careful reading of the first draft and numerous shrewd suggestions, my appreciation to: Joseph Coyle, Buz Hargraves, Lee Lacy, and Jon Keeton. David and Kathleen Hoopes and Peggy Pusch took over from them and did a splendid job of finetuning.

And for their efforts to shepherd this book carefully and efficiently through the vagaries of prepublication, my thanks to Helen Wattley Ames, Judy Carl Hendrick, and the other fine folks at Intercultural Press in Maine.

Finally, as always, my debt to my wife Charlotte—in ways too numerous to mention—is deep and lasting.

CRAIG STORTI
Washington, DC
January, 1989

Introduction

Now it is not good for the Christian's health
   to hustle the Aryan brown
For the Christian riles and the Aryan smiles and
   he weareth the Christian down.
And the end of the fight is a tombstone white
   with the name of the late deceased,
And the epitaph drear: "A fool lies here who
   tried to hustle the East."

        —RUDYARD KIPLING

I really don't know what happens next—one so
seldom does.

        —E. M. FORSTER
        The Hill of Devi

Many, perhaps most, people who go abroad to live and work genuinely want to adapt to the local culture. And most of them do not. It's not that they don't appreciate the reasons for adapting to the culture or know that it is all but essential to being successful in their work and at ease in the society, but rather that true cultural adjustment and effective cross-cultural interaction are more elusive than we might imagine. In this book we will explain why—and what to do about it.

The failure to adjust overseas and its attendant human, economic and political costs are well documented. According to a 1984 article in the *International Herald Tribune*, "More than one-third of all Americans who take up residence in foreign countries return prematurely because they are unable to adapt to day-to-day life."[1] The early return rate for Peace Corps volunteers has hovered for years between 10–20 percent. In Saudi Arabia an average of 68 percent of those Americans who have no cultural training fail to complete their contracts. In Western Europe, 37 percent of the Americans working on an F–16 project for General Dynamics resigned early and went home. Even in England, seemingly one of the easier countries for an American to live in, 18 percent of untrained American expatriates regularly return home prematurely. At one time an organization that recruited and placed hospital administrators in a Middle Eastern country reported an attrition rate of virtually 100 percent.

Nor should we assume that all those sojourners who do manage to stay abroad and complete their tour of duty have necessarily adapted to the culture. Indeed, as an extended visit in any foreign capital will prove, the percentage of expatriates who have not adjusted to the culture but remained in their assignments is, if anything, greater than the percentage of those who have gone home. Early return or failure rates, in short, are but one measure of the problem. It can be argued, in fact, that expatriates who "stick it out" are an even more serious problem (and potential expense to their employers) than those who leave. "The success rate of overseas adjustment among Americans is not nearly as high as it might be," Robert Kohls has observed in *Survival Kit for Overseas Living*. "If left to luck, your chances of having a satisfying experience living abroad would be about one in seven."[2]

The costs of unsuccessful adjustment are reckoned in myriad ways, but one of the easiest to quantify is the financial expense incurred by affected companies, institutions and governments. "The premature return of an overseas employee, a spouse, and two children can cost a company more than $210,000," estimates Lewis Griggs, co-producer of the "Going International" film series.[3] Every time one of its volunteers comes home early, the Peace Corps loses 50–75 percent of the estimated $7000 it costs the agency to recruit and train one worker.

But recruitment, training, and transportation expenses are only one measure of the cost. "Cross-cultural mistakes," Griggs observes, "can result in ruined careers, lost contracts, and re-duced productivity."[4] In a review of a biography of Saudi millionaire Adnan Khashoggi, Peter Collier notes that "Khashoggi's genius was to know how to play each side [U.S. arms merchants and the Saudi royal family and military] off against each other and how to take advantage of the misunderstandings and faux pas in cross-cultural negotiations."[5] General Motors lost untold sales when it made a classic cultural blunder by omitting to change the name of its Nova model when introducing the car into the company's South American market; "No va" means "it doesn't go" in Spanish. As the *Washington Post* has noted:

> The same bull-in-a-china-shop attitude toward foreign cultures and languages that has always cost American travelers respect overseas is now costing American business billions of dollars a year, according to experts.[6]

The U.S. Southern Governors' Association recently released a report decrying the "international illiteracy" that puts the United States "at a disadvantage with other countries in business and political affairs." The association commissioned the 1986 study because of the region's changing economy and dependence on foreign business. The South exported about $35 billion in manufactured products in 1984, making up about 30 percent of the country's manufacturing exports.[7] "Never before," said Virginia Governor Gerald Baliles, head of the Association's panel on international education, "has there been the economic motivation that exists now for Americans to understand and be knowledgeable about foreign customs and business procedures."[8]

Cultural blindness is not unique to Americans. The British were famous for it in their colonial empire and now the spotlight is increasingly on the Japanese. According to the *Spectator,* British employees in Japanese firms in London resent Japanese attitudes. One former employee of a Japanese banking house in London observed: "I felt as if all my knowledge was being squeezed out of me, like an orange. And they really do believe they are racially superior, and that we are no better than cats or dogs." In New York, the *Spectator* continues, one Japanese company's "habit of holding regular meetings which excluded American employees was one factor behind the recent walk-out of about thirty of the local staff."[9]

The failure of expatriates to understand and adjust to other cultures can have serious diplomatic, military and political consequences as well. The former deputy director of the CIA, Bobby Inman, blames agency operatives' "lack of deep understanding" of foreign societies for numerous "surprises" in international affairs. Neil Koch, a former deputy assistant secretary of defense, makes the same point in an article about North Korea. "The problem with American intelligence estimates," he writes,

> is that they are prepared by Americans. Our track record for piercing historical and cultural differences to arrive at accurate assessments of what an adversary might do is not enviable. [10]

In his review of *The Ayatollah in the Cathedral* by former Iran hostage Moorhead Kennedy, Jonathan Yardley notes that "the hostage crisis was a direct result—and had our policy makers been a bit more prescient, an entirely predictable one—of American ignorance of foreign cultures and history." [11] In an unsettling passage, Kennedy describes how our Foreign Service officers are neither particularly interested in nor encouraged to pursue cultural sensitivity:

> Granted the danger of seeing events entirely from the point of view of one's host country, there is the far more common danger of not understanding the local point of view at all. Far too many of our colleagues did not think such participation was necessary. Seeing only other Americans requires less effort. All they were interested in were "contacts," local people who would give them information. Nor did the Foreign Service rating system put much premium on how well one could enter into and understand a foreign society. By and large America's isolationist traditions, combined with an unfortunate self-centeredness, keep too many of our Foreign Service officers aloof from the foreign environment they work in. [12]

"We're Latins," Fidel Velazquez, the head of Mexico's largest and most powerful labor union, told an American journalist not long ago, "and our mentality is totally different from yours. We are further removed from material things than from those of the spirit. We are better able to bear poverty than mistreatment. If that were understood in the United States, we could be closer to you."[13]

Perhaps the most damaging of all are the human costs: the sense of failure, disappointment and loss of self-esteem on the part of the early returnee and his family, the stress and trauma of relocation, of finding a new job (in more extreme cases) and starting a new life. For those expatriates who stick it out, there are feelings of bitterness and anger (usually misdirected at the local people), a bunker mentality, and a dangerous shrinking of their capacity for sympathy and compassion—a narrowing of their humanity.

Nor are the costs borne exclusively by expatriates and their sponsoring institutions: they are felt by the local people as well. The villagers who are suddenly deprived of their Peace Corps health worker or the farmers served by the research station that just lost its expatriate crop specialist are just as affected by this change in their lives as the particular development workers involved.

The Art of Crossing Cultures is intended for all those going abroad—to live, work, or study—whose circumstances require them to interact effectively with the local people. While the illustrative anecdotes tend to feature Westerners living in non-Western societies, the underlying concepts apply to anyone who leaves a familiar culture to sojourn in a new one. The book will also be useful to those who work or otherwise have close contact with expatriates in their own country.

The words "adapt" and "adjust" are used interchangeably throughout the book and are intended to mean the process of learning the new culture and its behaviors and language in an effort to understand and empathize with the people of the culture, and to live among and interact successfully with them. Those expatriates who choose to become less involved in the local culture will find many useful insights in this book but it is really intended for those who wish to become fully engaged with members of the host culture. Thus it is written from the perspective that adjusting to the local (foreign) culture is valuable, desirable, and greatly enhances one's experience abroad.

In chapter 1 we look briefly at some of the difficulties of adjusting to another *country*. While this is not our theme in these pages—and is not to be confused with adjusting to a new *culture*—adjustment to country and culture go on simultaneously, with success in the former often purchased at the expense of progress in the latter.

In chapter 2 we present the **problem,** defining and giving examples of the two main kinds of adjustments sojourners must make. Chapter 3 chronicles how most expatriates go wrong, explaining how maladjustment occurs and why it is so common. Chapter 4 unearths the **cause,** explaining why it is we find other cultures so difficult to get used to, and chapter 5 offers a **solution,** a technique for adapting successfully.

Chapters 6, 7 and 8, respectively, expand on concepts introduced earlier: we look at certain aspects of adjustment more closely, consider the influence of learning the local language on the experience of living abroad, and describe some of the consequences of reaching our goal. And chapter 9 deals with the question of readjustment to one's own culture after the sojourn is over.

It is impossible to describe in detail how expatriates grapple with the difficulties of crossing cultures without making the overseas experience sound rather grim and tiresome—all work and no reward. It isn't that way, of course. The benefits and delights of a sojourn in a foreign country are numerous and profound, but they generally don't require any getting used to. Our purpose in these pages is not to slight the rewards of living abroad—even if at times we may seem to—but to help the sojourner understand and take control of the experience and thereby render it all the richer.

REFERENCES

1. *International Herald Tribune,* 15 August 1984.

2. L. Robert Kohls, *Survival Kit for Overseas Living* (Yarmouth, Maine: Intercultural Press, 1984), 2.

3. *International Herald Tribune,* 15 August 1984.

4. Ibid.

5. Peter Collier, review of *The Richest Man in the World: The Story of Adnan Khashoggi*, by Ronald Kessler, *Washington Post* "Book World," 20 July 1986.

6. *International Herald Tribune*, 15 August 1986.

7. *Washington Post*, 22 November 1986.

8. Ibid.

9. Dominic Lawson, "Softly, Softly Catchee Market," *Spectator*, October 1987.

10. *Washington Post* "Outlook," date unknown.

11. Jonathan Yardley, review of *The Ayatollah in the Cathedral*, by Moorhead Kennedy, *Washington Post* "Book World, 20 July 1986.

12. Moorhead Kennedy, *The Ayatollah in the Cathedral* (New York: Hill and Wang, 1986), 34–35.

13. "The Most Powerful Man in Mexico." *Washington Post*, op. ed. page, 1987, month and day unknown.

■ 1 ■

THE HOWLING OF TIGERS, THE HISSING OF SERPENTS

Nor did he like . . . the heat and the dirt and the everpresent threat of tapeworms and other even more disagreeable parasites.

—FITZROY MACLEAN
A Person from England and Other Travellers

I should say, looking back calmly upon the matter, that seventy-five percent of West African insects sting, five percent bite, and the rest are either prematurely or temporarily parasitic on the human race. And undoubtedly one of the worst things you can do in West Africa is to take any notice of an insect. If you see a thing that looks like a cross between a flying lobster and a figure of Abraxes on a Gnostic gem, do not pay it the least attention, never mind where it is; just keep quiet and hope it will go away—for that's your best chance; you have none in a stand-up fight with a good, thorough-going African insect.

—MARY KINGSLEY
West African Studies

Kynna kept a cheerful countenance, but felt her spirits flag. The alien speech of the passersby, the

inscrutable monuments, the unknown landscape,
the vanishing of all she had pictured in advance,
were draining her of certainty. . . . She had
known the world was vast, but at home in her
native hills it had had no meaning. Now, on the
threshold of the illimitable East, she felt like a
desolation its indifferent strangeness.

—MARY RENAULT
Funeral Games

It is so very HOT I do not know how to write it
large enough.

—EMILY EDEN
Up the Country

Before you can adapt to foreign culture, you first have to survive
the move abroad. People who move overseas face a number of
adjustments all at once. They must, of course, come to grips
with the local culture, with the peculiar behavior of the natives. But they must also get used to a new job, a new community, and a new country. While our focus in this work is on
cultural adjustment, these other adjustments deserve attention,
for they are very much a part of the overall context in which
the process of *cultural* adaptation takes place—or does not. Oc-
curring at the same time as cultural adaptation and competing
for the sojourners' attention and energy (neither of which are
unlimited) adjusting to job, community and country inevitably
affect the pace—and the outcome—of the expatriates' struggle
to make sense out of the culture around them. The impact of
these challenges is so direct and immediate that if the problems
they pose aren't acknowledged and addressed early on, the resulting stress and anxiety can overwhelm and defeat the sojourners before they ever really encounter the culture. In short,
while dealing effectively with what we might call these lesser
adjustments may not constitute cultural adaptation, it could determine whether such adaptation ever comes to pass.

What, then, does adjusting to a new job entail? It will certainly involve learning and adapting to the various policies and

office procedures of the new workplace, from figuring out how to submit a travel claim to remembering which files belong in locked file cabinets and which do not. There is the history of the organization or project to learn and key program or policy issues to be grasped. There may also be new areas of responsibility to master (in the case of a promotion) or entirely new skills to acquire. And there will be any number of new people to meet and learn to work with. It will be six to nine months before you feel comfortable and confident in the job, confident enough, let's say, to propose improvements or changes in the organization or suggest initiatives—in other words, to make the kind of substantive contribution most satisfying to a professional. It is disconcerting (in the best of circumstances) to be at the top of your form one moment—as you probably were in your last months at your previous job—and all thumbs the next.

Then there are the adjustments to the new community. You have to learn your way around, find out the location and business hours of a variety of shops and services, and determine which shops carry which goods. You have to crack the code of the taxi and bus systems, learn what to do in an emergency, and find out where it is safe to go and where it is not. We take so much for granted about the places where we live, we forget that we once had to learn all we know.

We come now to the country. The most immediate adjustment the expatriate must make is to the new climate. Winter in Kathmandu can be physically (and emotionally) traumatic to someone raised in southern California, just as April in Sri Lanka can be discouraging to a New Englander. ("I've been in Ceylon a month," wrote D. H. Lawrence, "and nearly sweated myself into a shadow."[1]) A sudden, dramatic change in climate—the legacy of air travel—may be just what the planeload of sunworshipping Scandinavians is looking for, but it is quite another matter for the expatriate; the weather can wreak havoc on the body and lifestyle of those unaccustomed to it. The tourist pays good money for this havoc; the sojourner must learn to live with it.

To one unaccustomed to it, the heat of the tropics can be debilitating. For the first few weeks, even months, one feels a marked loss of energy, a need for more sleep, and any number of symptoms commonly associated with dehydration, such as head-

aches and low-grade fevers. "Things have improved," E. M. Forster wrote when he was on the mend in India. "I feel more alert
and able to concentrate. The heat made me so stupid and
sleepy."[2]

You may have to scrap plans to walk or bicycle to work (thus
leaving your spouse home without a car), give up tennis on your
lunch hour, and buy new clothes. You may gain weight because
you don't get enough exercise or your skin may break out, causing you to become depressed about your appearance. "As she
made up her face," Anthony Burgess writes of an expatriate wife
in Malaysia, "cursing the sweat that clogged the powder, she was
sick for London, coolly making up for a dance in the evening,
or for the ballet or for a concert. Civilization is only possible in
a temperate zone."[3] "The humidity," Burgess writes elsewhere in
The Long Day Wanes (see appendix 2), "could be blamed for
many things: the need for a siesta, corpulence, the use of the
car for a hundred-yard journey, the mildew on the shoes, the
sweatrot in the armpits of dresses, the lost bridge-rubber or
tennis-set, the dislike felt for the whole country."[4]

Too cold is no improvement on too hot. Winter nights in
Kathmandu hover just above freezing, yet no house in the city
has central heating (nor, for that matter, do most homes in England built before 1950). You can heat a room or two (when the
power is on), but you won't be able to heat the house. And
from being cold to catching a cold, needless to say, is a short
step.

Then there is the monsoon which occurs each year throughout much of Asia and the Pacific: two to three months of relentless rain that makes you a prisoner in your own home, flooded,
impassable streets and roads, mold sprouting on your shoes and
clothes and creeping down the walls, relentless rain that makes
you a prisoner in your own home. At least in the hot weather
you can still go outside and move about, but in the monsoon
you have no desire (though you don't want to be inside either).
Like excessive heat and cold, the monsoon not only makes you
uncomfortable, it can make you unhappy.

Poor communications is another cross the expatriate (in less
developed countries) frequently has to bear. In many places telephones, in the home or the office, are a luxury, and even where
they can be had, the system is often so old or overloaded as to

be in perpetual disrepair. Imagine for a moment having to go to all, or even half, of the places you telephone on an average day from work or from home. Without telephones, or with very few telephones, the amount of business an aid worker can conduct in Lahore or Kandy may be half what he or she is used to (while the effort may be double). In the West the telephone is like a third hand; naturally, when all at once it's amputated, you miss it.

The absence of telephones is at least part of the reason for the expatriate's favorite complaint about how long it takes to get things done in developing countries, and it likewise goes a long way toward explaining that other old standby about the slower pace of life in Asia or Latin America or around the shores of the Mediterranean. People have more time for each other, we hear; they enjoy each other's company more. While personal relationships are certainly more important in many countries than in the West, the fact is when you can't call, you have to go, and a visit invariably takes longer and is inevitably more personal than a phone call. No one thinks it odd if you hang up after three minutes, but if you leave three minutes after arriving at someone's home or office (when you spent half an hour just to get there) the effect would be rather startling.

A related problem is poor transportation. If you can't call—and the problem can't wait—then you must go. In Sri Lanka it is seventy-five miles from Colombo to Galle. If you leave at 8:30 A.M. for a ten o'clock appointment, you'll be late by two hours. If you need a spare part in Pokhara (Nepal) and it has to come from Kathmandu, ninety miles away, you can take off the rest of the day.

"It was not like other bad roads," Peter Fleming writes in *Brazilian Adventure*,

> which incommode you with continuous and petty malice. "Look how far we can go," they seem to say, as you crawl painfully along them, "and still be called a road." You hate them the more bitterly for the knowledge that they will keep certain bounds. They will madden you with minor obstacles, but in the end they will let you through.
>
> But with the road to Leopoldina it was not like this. It had no quarrel with us. It took no count of us at

all. It did not fight a sly, delaying action, raising our
hopes only to dash them, but always keeping them
alive. It did not set out to tantalize us or gall us. It
seemed, rather, preoccupied with its own troubles. It
had never wished to be a road, and now it cursed
itself for not refusing its function before it was too
late. It lashed itself into a fury of self-reproach. It
writhed in anguish. It was clearly a tormented thing.
At any moment, we felt, it might decide to End it
All.[5]

Yet another irritation overseas is having to do without.
Wherever you go, but especially in developing countries, the
list of things "they don't have here" seems diabolic: no mush-
rooms, oregano, or fresh cream; no presifted flour (or a flour
sifter), no decent thread, no shoes that fit or vacuum cleaner
bags; matches, or batteries; no Ektachrome ASA 400. And
some of the things you can't get—good films, English books and
newspapers, television—strip you of many of your preferred pas-
times.

Tiresome as the above frustrations can be, surely the most
inconvenient—and fearful—problem the expatriate must face is
the near constant threat of getting sick. No other difficulty can
be quite so unsettling nor require more time and effort to cir-
cumvent. You might reasonably suppose that expatriate party
talk revolves around issues of moment, such as the declining
peso or forecasts of another year of drought, but it touches just
as often on the solidity of one's stools and how long to soak the
lettuce. This is only natural: while you can learn to manage
without a telephone or a TV or central heating, you can't do
anything if you're confined to bed. And the combination of the
amoebas and parasites lurking in the food and water of many
developing countries and the pristine vulnerability of the expatriate from the antiseptic, sterilized West virtually guarantees
that, feverish and cramp-ridden, it is to bed we will retire more
than once during those early months abroad.

But the worst part about being sick overseas is not what it
does to the body, but what it does to the mind. You become
depressed. Your resolve weakens. Doubt arises. "Through most
of his experience of the rains," Paul Scott writes of a character
newly arrived in India, "he was chronically and depressingly off-

colour. Whatever he ate turned his bowels to water. In such circumstances a human being goes short on courage."[6] If I hadn't come here, you can't help feeling, none of this would have happened.

Most disturbing of all about trying to establish yourself in a new environment is not knowing anyone. Little in life is more unsettling than change, facing the unknown; and one of the few factors that can mitigate the feelings of insecurity which change provokes is the support of close friends and loved ones, of those who stand by you—who do *not* change even as everything else around you seems to. The homesickness sojourners feel so acutely during their early weeks abroad is not so much a longing to see certain old friends and family members again as it is a longing to experience once again the support and comfort of friendship itself. It is not so much a desire to *be* back home as a desire to *feel at home* in the new surroundings. It is not impossible to go through the changes described above without the support of others, but the absence of such support only makes the experience more intense and aggravates already keen feelings of isolation, loneliness and self-doubt.

The impact of so much that is new and unfamiliar seriously disrupts your life. You find yourself becoming more and more absorbed in the minutiae of day-to-day existence as you are forced by your new circumstances to give close attention to things you are used to taking for granted. "Ordinary everyday situations," Adrian Furnham and Stephen Bochner have observed in *Cultures in Conflict,*

> such as attending parties, making contact with the opposite sex, ordering meals, shopping, even using the bathroom, all activities which hitherto presented no problems, suddenly become major obstacles. . . . Individuals in this predicament include foreign students, visiting academics, businessmen, and diplomats [who] tend to be highly skilled . . . in their own society, and [therefore] find their inadequacy in the new culture particularly frustrating and embarrassing.[7]

Work and personal habits have to be altered. Everything takes longer and seems to require an additional step. If you are making a salad, you have to remember to start soaking the lettuce twenty minutes ahead of time. If you are making a purchase at a small shop, you will probably have to get change somewhere first. "Cashing a traveller's check in Trebizond," one writer has observed, "takes two banks an entire morning and involves the police."[8]

What you are experiencing is the phenomenon popularly known as culture shock (though *country* shock is what we really mean). In isolation, none of the difficulties mentioned above would be so taxing, but when they are encountered in the aggregate, which is invariably the case, the time and energy they consume can be considerable.

"I have already mentioned," writes Captain John Stedman of his 1772 journey through Surinam,

> the prickly heat, ringworm, dry gripes, putrid fevers, biles, consaca, and bloody flux, to which human nature is exposed in this climate; also the mosquitoes, Patat and Scrapat lice, chigoes, cockroaches, ants, horseflies, wild bees and bats, besides the thorns and briars, and the alligators and peree in the rivers; to which if we add the howling of tigers, the hissing of serpents, and the growling of Four-geoud, the dry, sandy savannahs, unfordable marshes, burning hot days, cold and damp nights, heavy rains, and short allowance, the reader may be astonished how any person was able to survive the trial. Notwithstanding this black catalogue, I solemnly declare I have omitted many other calamities that we suffered, as I wish to avoid prolixity.[9]

Naturally, you begin to feel cornered, frustrated, and at times overwhelmed by all you have to contend with. The upshot is that you spend much of your time during these early months abroad simply trying to cope. This isn't beyond your reach, but mere coping can be demoralizing as it leaves little time or energy for more fulfilling, meaningful pursuits, such as learning about and appreciating the new country, learning the local language, or making a contribution in your new job. And it was, after all, the possibility of this latter kind of achievement—rather than successfully mailing a letter—that attracted you to going abroad in the first place.

What, then, are we to do about this "black catalogue"? How are we to withstand the stresses of moving overseas? To begin with, it helps immensely to know these stresses are coming. If we expect something of a rough ride, we aren't caught altogether off our guard. We may still be thrown by the experience, but being psychologically prepared diminishes the impact.

We should also remind ourselves that the stress and anxiety we feel are entirely normal. We have, after all, set ourselves an ambitious agenda. Indeed, it would be unusual, and a cause for some concern, if we *didn't* feel anxious in our situation. We should be careful not to deny that we may be feeling frustrated or lonely or inadequate. Admitting these feelings to ourselves, and especially to others, helps reduce them. If, for whatever reason, we are obliged to keep a stiff upper lip in public, we should at least permit ourselves a quivering one in the privacy of our home.

It also helps to keep our trials in perspective and not take them too seriously. We aren't in any danger, after all; the diseases we are prey to are rarely the life-threatening variety. Moreover, we should remember that we have been through all this (or at least much of it) before (if never quite on this scale), when we changed jobs, moved, or were separated from family and friends on other occasions in our lives and lived to tell the tale. And we should remember, too, that our circumstances—and our feelings *about* our circumstances—will change.

We should also try to be precise about the source of our frustrations. Some of our trials are new, the result of our changed environment and circumstances, and may require original solutions. But many others are simply old trials turning up in a new place. As such, we already know what to do about them (i.e., the same thing we did the last time), provided, that is, we identify them for what they are. On the whole, life doesn't pose that many new dilemmas; it merely recycles the same ones in new packaging.

In addition to cultivating the proper attitude, there are some specific actions we can take to ease the stress of adjusting to a new country. The first and most important is to look after our health. We have no control over much of what happens to us during our early months abroad, but we can control what we eat and how much exercise and sleep we get.

We should also make an effort to keep in touch with family and friends back home, to write or call regularly. We are bound to become lonely and homesick in a new country—that is in the nature of a sojourn—but we can at least control the degree of loneliness we experience.

Similarly, we should seek out other people. The tendency, when we feel depressed or inadequate, is to keep to ourselves. We are bad company, we reason, and shouldn't inflict our low spirits on others. But this only feeds our depression. By being with and responding to others we are obliged to come out of our preoccupation, to turn our attention away from our anxieties. And this can only be therapeutic. Moreover, we may discover that it's not just us, that others are having the same reactions and doubts.

Above all, we must be patient. Appreciating the scale and variety of the adjustments we face, we should not expect too much of ourselves. We should be content, for the moment, with small successes. Our goal should be to function, not to triumph.

With patience, persistence and intelligence there is no reason the average expatriate cannot learn to function effectively and easily in a new country. But a word of caution: we must be careful not to confuse adjusting to the new country (and the job and community) with adapting to or understanding the culture. The growing sense of well-being and self-confidence we feel as we begin to adapt to our surroundings can blind us to the true nature of our achievement. Simply because we've gotten used to the food or figured out the bus routes doesn't mean we understand the culture. Getting used to curry isn't the same as getting used to the people who eat curry. It is a relief to begin to feel comfortable in our new surroundings, but that doesn't mean they can no longer surprise us.

Meanwhile, it won't do to be morose about all this. What if it is tedious running around Monrovia because the phones are out again or learning to live without central heating or *Dallas*? Isn't this what we came for—for something different, the occasional adventure, a dash of risk and hardship? Surely we don't pull up our roots and take ourselves and our families halfway around the world in the hope that everything will be exactly as it is back home. "This is royal," Mark Twain wrote upon arriving in Morocco,

> We wanted something thoroughly and uncompromis-
> ingly foreign—foreign from top to bottom—foreign
> from center to circumference—foreign inside and
> outside and all around—nothing anywhere about it
> to dilute its foreignness—nothing to remind us of
> any other people or any other land under the sun.
> And lo! In Tangiers we have found it.[10]

Where is the sense of accomplishment if there are no obstacles to surmount? How can we learn and grow from our experiences if we don't have any? "You have to be able to sustain
reversals, upsets, accidents," notes Philip Glazebrook in his excellent *Journey to Kars* (see appendix 2),

> Things going wrong gives you the chance to show
> self-reliance; and isn't the assertion of self-reliance
> one of the chief objects of independent travel? If I'd
> really been separated from my [bags], a couple of
> days of dogged ingenuity would have been needed to
> reunite me with them, but it could have been done,
> and if I'd achieved it, I'd have felt extremely pleased
> with myself.[11]

Lord Byron would have agreed. He once ranked life's pursuits
and concluded that gambling, battle, and travel were the fore-
most. Their "particular attraction," he noted, lay in "the agitation inseparable from their accomplishment. [They make us] feel
that we exist."[12]

REFERENCES

1. D. H. Lawrence, *Letters*, excerpted in Hugh and Pauline Massingham, comps., *The Englishman Abroad* (Gloucester, UK:
   Alan Sutton, 1984), 25.

2. E. M. Forster, *The Hill of Devi* (New York: Penguin, 1983), 91.

3. Anthony Burgess, *The Long Day Wanes: A Malayan Trilogy*
   (New York: W. W. Norton & Co., 1964), 56.

4. Ibid., 36.

5. Peter Fleming, *Brazilian Adventure* excerpted in John Julius
   Norwich, ed., *A Taste for Travel* (London: Macmillan, 1985),
   126.

6. Paul Scott, *The Jewel in the Crown* (New York: Avon, 1979), 245.

7. Stephen Bochner and Adrian Furnham, "Social Difficulty in Foreign Cultures: An Empirical Analysis of Culture Shock," in Stephen Bucher, ed., *Cultures in Conflict* (Oxford: Pergamon Press, 1982), 166.

8. R. Z. Sheppard, review of *Journey to Kars* by Philip Glazebrook, in *Time*, 26 November 1984.

9. John Stedman, *Expedition to Surinam*, excerpted in John Julius Norwich, ed., *A Taste for Travel* (London: Macmillan, 1985), 229.

10. Mark Twain, *The Innocents Abroad* (New York: The New American Library, 1966), 57.

11. Philip Glazebrook, *Journey to Kars* (New York: Penguin, 1984), 20.

12. Paul Fussell, ed., *The Norton Book of Travel* (New York: W. W. Norton, 1987), 14.

■ 2 ■
MAD DOGS AND ENGLISHMEN

There is nothing so vile or repugnant to nature, but you may plead prescription for it in the customs of some nation or other. A Parisian likes mortified flesh; a native of Legiboli will not taste his fish until it is quite putrefied; the civilized inhabitants of Kamschatka get drunk with the urine of their guests, whom they have already intoxicated; the Nova Zemblans make merry on train oil; the Greenlanders eat in the same dish as their dogs; the Caffres, at the Cape of Good Hope, piss upon those whom they delight to honor, and feast upon a sheep's intestines with their contents, as the greatest dainty that can be presented.

—TOBIAS SMOLLETT
Travels through France and Italy

What strikes me the most upon the whole is the total difference of manners between them and us, from the greatest object to the least. There is not the smallest similitude in the twenty-four hours. It is obvious in every trifle.

—HORACE WALPOLE
Letters

In chapter 1, we discussed the adjustments the sojourner must make to the new job, new community, and the new country.

Our focus now, and in the remainder of this book, is on how to adapt to culture. In a way, of course, culture is part of country, but we have used *country* here in the narrow sense, to mean the physical circumstances—climate, communication and transportation systems, health conditions, isolation. Country is the locale, the setting of culture, but culture itself, as we use it here, refers to people and how they behave.

"All people are the same," Confucius said. "It's only their habits that are different." People's habits and how to get used to them are the subject of this book. We speak of *cultural* adjustment, but in fact it is not to culture that we adjust but to behavior. Culture, a system of beliefs and values shared by a particular group of people, is an abstraction which can be appreciated intellectually, but it is behavior, the principal manifestation and most significant consequence of culture, that we actually experience. To put it another way: it is culture as encountered in behavior that we must learn to live with.

It is not Islam that annoys us—most of us know very little about it—but the actions of our Moslem landlord. We don't have to adjust to Buddhism, but it behooves us to try to understand our Buddhist gardener or our Buddhist colleagues at work.

Behavior, then, is our subject. But not *all* behavior. While it is in behavior that we experience—and express—culture, not all behavior is rooted in culture. Many of our actions—caring for our children, communicating through language—are inherently human, the common property of our species and unchanging from culture to culture, what Confucius meant when he said, "All people are the same."

At the opposite end of the continuum is the behavior which is unique to each individual, rooted in personal experience. It is this behavior which allows us to distinguish individuals within a particular culture. Our landlord behaves in certain ways because he's a Moslem (and that's his culture) and in other ways because he's Hassan, second son of Ali and Khadija, raised by his grandmother in the village of Tetouan, where the family moved when he was three.

Nearly all Americans eat three meals a day: one in the morning, one at midday, and one in the evening. This is cultural behavior. But some people have cereal for breakfast, others toast; some have a light lunch and a full dinner, others vice versa; some people eat in the dining room (at least when company comes), others in the living room with the TV playing. These are individual behaviors, personal variations on a cultural theme. "People say she was unlike other English people," an Indian man remarks in Paul Scott's *The Day of the Scorpion*:

> I do not know what they mean when they are saying
> that. English people are not mass-produced. They do
> not come off a factory line all looking, speaking,
> thinking, acting the same. Neither do we.[1]

We will have occasion to refer to these two categories of behavior in a later chapter, but for the present our focus is on neither the ways in which all people are alike nor the ways in which each of us is unique, but on what happens when one group of people behaves very oddly in the eyes of another.

The adjustments we must make to a new culture are invariably of two kinds: we have to adjust or get used to behavior on the part of the local people which annoys, confuses, or otherwise unsettles us; and we have to adjust our own behavior so that it does not annoy, confuse, or otherwise unsettle the local people. So long as we are put off by or consistently misconstrue the behavior of the locals and so long as we repeatedly provoke or baffle the locals by our own behavior, we can never expect to feel at ease abroad or to be wholly effective in our work. In this chapter we will present examples of these two kinds of problems, which we will refer to as *Type I* and *Type II*. In succeeding chapters we will examine the underlying causes of these two dilemmas, propose a solution to them, and outline a technique for putting that solution in practice in our day-to-day lives.

We begin with an assortment of Type I incidents, those in which the behavior of the natives is giving us, the expatriates, cause for concern.

A study of Westerners in Japan conducted by Waseda University's department of psychology found that peculiarities of Japanese behavior contributed to the culture shock that made foreigners ill. Among the complaints of foreigners

were the Japanese habits of urinating on the
street, smiling with no particular reason,
excessive attention to cleanliness, slurping soup,
and staring at foreigners.

—*Manchester Guardian*

But the chief confusion for outsiders was that [the
natives] telescoped time. They would relate
something that happened five years ago as if it
happened last week, and so you could go very
badly astray on this.

—CHARLES ALLEN
Tales from the South China Seas

When they came they often brought singers and
musicians to entertain me. The only hitch was
[the Moroccans] went to such lengths to treat me
as one of them that they also assumed I was not
interested in going out into the city. During the
entire fortnight I spent with them I never once
found my way out of the house. For long hours I
sat in the patio listening to the sounds of the city
outside, in the hope that someone would come,
something would happen. But as I say, if I was
bored, that was my own fault. They were doing
everything they could to please me.

—PAUL BOWLES
Their Heads Are Green and Their Hands Are Blue

I walked through the city this morning . . . but
before I had gone very far I began to feel
timid. . . . I found myself an object of curiosity,
and this embarrassed me. Everyone stared at me;
people who were squatting on their heels in front
of their houses rose up, salaamed, called others
out and stood staring; groups of men interrupted
their conversation to watch me pass; children

followed me, and women covered their faces. . . .
I felt intrusive and self-conscious.

—J. R. ACKERLEY
Hindoo Holiday

Nothing is more charming than southern
courtesy, but sometimes they really are too
sympathetic by half. For in order not to
contradict you or give you a moment's pain by
disputing the accuracy of your ideas, they will tell
you what you want to hear rather than what
would be of real use to you to hear. At the same
time their own self-esteem will not permit them
to confess a blank ignorance; they will rather
tell you something incorrect than tell you
nothing at all.

—ALDOUS HUXLEY
Along the Road

"I am not the type, monsieur, who feels himself
superior to the rest of humanity. Indeed, I am no
better than others. But these people, these
Afghans. They are not human."
"But why do you say that?"
"You don't see why, monsieur? Have you eyes?
Look at those men over there. Are they not
eating with their hands? With their hands! It is
frightful."

—ROBERT BYRON
The Road to Oxiana

One of the terms most frequently used by
Americans to describe the Japanese *modus
operandi* is the word "indirection." An American
banker who had just spent years in Japan and
made the minimum possible accommodation told
me that what he found most frustrating and
difficult was their indirection. "An old-style

17

Japanese," he complained, "can drive a man crazy faster than anything I know. They talk around and around and around a point and never do get to it."

Americans living in England . . . are hurt and puzzled because they were brought up on American neighboring patterns and don't interpret the English ones correctly. In England propinquity means nothing. The fact that you live next door to a family does not entitle you to visit, borrow from or socialize with them, or your children to play with theirs.

I was once called in to advise [an American] firm that has operations all over the world. One of the first questions they asked was, "How do you get Germans to keep their doors open?" Closed doors gave the Americans the feeling that there was a conspiratorial air about the place and that they were being left out.

> —EDWARD T. HALL
> *The Hidden Dimension*

Indians do seem uncouth to the European. I shared the compartment with fat Mr. Jain, a vegetarian with swollen lips of the kind known as sensual, mouth and teeth red-stained from betel juice, who punctuated the dark hours with snores and farts and hawkings—all Indians appear to do this. Yesterday morning an American family was having breakfast with their guide who, in mid-conversation, gave vent to an elaborate hawking and clearing of the passages; they regarded their cornflakes expressionlessly.

> —J. G. FARRELL
> *Indian Diary*

In this arrangement of the day no circumstance is so objectionable as that of dining at noon . . .

for as the ceremony of dressing is kept up, you
must be home from any morning's excursion by
twelve o'clock. . . . Dividing the day exactly in
halves destroys it for any expedition, business, or
enquiry that demands seven or eight hours'
attention. . . . I am induced to make this
observation because the noon dinners are
customary all over France. They cannot be
treated with too much ridicule or severity for they
are hostile to every view of science, to every
spirited exertion, and to every useful pursuit
in life.

—ARTHUR YOUNG
Travels in France

The men walked hand-in-hand, laughing sleepily
together under blinding vertical glare. Sometimes
they put their arms round each other's necks;
they seemed to like to touch each other, as if it
made them feel good to know the other man was
there. It wasn't love; it didn't mean anything we
could understand.

—GRAHAM GREENE
Journey without Maps

The Russians' lack of personal space at home in
their apartments, on public transportation or on
the job causes them to erect their personal space-
boundaries next to their skin. Therefore it is
common for Russians to have deadpan or frozen
expressions on their faces. We tend to perceive
this as unfriendly and it may ruffle our feathers.

—JAN L. PERKOWSKI
America 4 October 1986

These, then, are examples of behavior to which the expatriate must learn to adapt. Or, more precisely, it is the failure to
adapt to incidents such as these that seriously undermines the

effectiveness and happiness of the sojourner in a foreign country. In a moment we will examine the dangers that lurk in these incidents, why, in short, something needs to be *done* about them. But first we offer a few examples of the second kind of adjustment the expatriate faces, what we are calling Type II incidents, wherein it is the sojourner who is behaving boorishly and the natives who are put off. In one sense these incidents are, of course, more of a problem for the natives than for us, for they are the ones being offended or frustrated. But in a larger sense the problem is ours: we cannot expect to be very effective abroad if we consistently alienate the people among whom we've come to live and work.

> It appeared that in walking through Tabiang the day before, [a foreigner] had passed between two women—the wife and daughter of an elder—as they were chatting to each other across the road. Seeing them in conversation, he should have stopped before crossing their line of vision and asked permission to go on. There was a proper formula for that: "*E matauninga te aba?* (Are the people offended?)" Had he used it, he would have been assured at once that nobody could be the least bit offended. But even then it would have been proper for him to pass forward with head and shoulders bowed well below their eye-line. His omission of these formalities had been the more astounding to the people because of his exalted rank among them.
>
> —ARTHUR GRIMBLE
> *A Pattern of Islands*

> Tourists stare at [Moroccans] in the Grand Soco, wondering, perhaps, what odd Johnnies they are, never suspecting that the scrutiny is reciprocal. With our sun-scorched foreheads, our bikini-in-the-street shamelessness, what can they think?
>
> —MICHAEL WATKINS
> *Times* (London) 19 March 1983

20

Americans tend to like people who agree with
them. Australians are more apt to be interested
in a person who disagrees with them; disagreement
is a basis for a lively conversation . . . and in
fact can indicate real interest and respect. The
average Australian wants to probe the American's
wit and resilience. While the American is
seeking a topic to chat about, the Australian is
seeking a partner to spar with. Thus, the
Australian finds the American boring.

—*English Teaching Forum*
October 1985

My first shock came when I was requested,
politely but firmly, by the guest-master to remove
a pair of underpants then fluttering happily from
the line. This, he pointed out, was a monastery;
shirts, socks, handkerchiefs, even vests, might be
dried with propriety within its walls. But
underpants were a shameful abomination and
could on no account be permitted. Meekly, I
obeyed; but worse was to come. I woke the
following morning at dawn . . . and made quietly
for the wash-house. Its principal furnishing was a
huge stone trough; and into this I now clambered,
covering myself from head to foot in a deep and
luxurious lather. At this point the guest-master
appeared. Never have I seen anyone so angry. For
the second time in twelve hours I had desecrated
his monastery. Having already offended God and
the Mother of God with the spectacle of my
underpants, I was now compounding the sacrilege
by standing stark naked under the very roof of
the Grand Lavra. I was the whore of Babylon, I
was Sodom and Gomorrah, I was a minion of
Satan sent to corrupt the Holy Mountain. I was
to put on my scabrous clothes at once and return
with all speed to the foul pit whence I had come.

—**JOHN JULIUS NORWICH**
Mount Athos

21

To the Arab good smells are pleasing and a way
of being involved with each other. To smell one's
friend is not only nice but desirable, for to deny
him your breath is to act ashamed. Americans,
on the other hand, trained as they are not to
breathe in people's faces, automatically
communicate shame in trying to be polite.

—EDWARD T. HALL
The Hidden Dimension

[The women of the harem] pitied us European
women heartily, that we had to go about
travelling, and appearing in the streets without
being properly taken care of—that is, watched.
They think us strangely neglected in being left so
free, and boast of [how closely they are watched]
as a token of the value in which they are held.

—HARRIET MARTINEAU
Eastern Life

I was travelling with a few of the nobles by train.
Seeing "Beef" on the menu, I ordered it. The
waiter said Beef was off, so I had something else.
Later, back in Dewas, the Maharajah said to me,
with great gentleness, "Morgan, I want to speak
to you on a very serious subject indeed. When
you were travelling with my people you asked to
eat something, the name of which I cannot even
mention. If the waiter had brought it, they would
all have had to leave the table. So they spoke to
him behind your back and told him to tell you
that it was not there. They did this because they
knew you did not intend anything wrong, and
because they love you."

—E. M FORSTER
The Hill of Devi

A major international blunder was successfully
avoided when Nancy Reagan revised her earlier

22

determination to take her White House china on
a state visit to the People's Republic of China in
1984. [The People's Republic was offended by the
implication that it, of all countries, might be
deficient in this regard.] However, unwittingly,
President Reagan managed to offend a shopkeeper
by asking him to "keep the change" after paying
for a small souvenir, an insult in a country where
tips are reserved for lowly servants.

—U.S. DEPT OF HEALTH/HUMAN SERVICES
Crossing Cultures

A little golden girl of seven . . . brought in a
coconut which she had opened under the tree
outside, sat down, and offered it to me cupped in
both hands, at arm's length, with her head a
little bowed. "You shall be blessed," she
murmured as I took it. I did say, "Thank you" in
reply, but even after that I should have returned
her blessing word for word, and after that I
should have returned the nut also, for her to take
the first sip of courtesy; and at last—when I
received it back, I should have said "Blessings
and Peace" before beginning to drink the milk.
All I did—woe is me!—was to take it, swig it
off, hand it back one-handed, empty, with
another careless, "Thank you."

"Alas," she said at last in a shocked whisper,
"Alas! Is that the manners of a young chief of
[the white people]?" She told me one by one the
sins I have confessed . . . but that was not the
full tale. My final discourtesy had been the
crudest of all. In handing back the empty nut, I
had omitted to belch aloud. "How could I know
when you did not belch . . . that my food was
sweet to you? See, this is how you should have
done it!" She held the nut towards me with both
hands, her earnest eyes fixed on mine, and gave
vent to a belch so resonant that it seemed to
shake her elfin form from stem to stern. "That,"

23

she finished, "is our idea of good manners," and
wept for the pity of it.

—ARTHUR GRIMBLE
A Pattern of Islands

In tropical climes there are certain times of day
When all the citizens retire
To tear off their clothes and perspire.
It's one of those rules that the greatest fools obey,
Because the sun is much too sultry
And one must avoid its ultry violet ray . . .
But mad dogs and Englishmen
Go out in the midday sun . . .

In the Philippines
There are lovely screens
To protect you from the glare.
In the Malay States
There are hats like plates
Which the Britishers won't wear.
At twelve noon
The natives swoon
And no further work is done.
But mad dogs and Englishmen
Go out in the midday sun.

The toughest Burmese bandit
Can never understand it.
In Rangoon the heat of noon
Is just what the natives shun . . .
In Bangkok
At twelve o'clock
They foam at the mouth and run.
But mad dogs and Englishmen
Go out in the midday sun.

—NOEL COWARD
Collected Lyrics

We might consider as well the apocryphal story of the American couple invited to a Moroccan family's home for dinner.

Having pressed their host to fix a time, they arrive half an hour late and are shown into the guest room. After a decent interval, they ask after the host's wife, who has yet to appear, and are told that she's busy in the kitchen. At one point their host's little son wanders in, and the couple remark on his good looks. Just before the meal is served, the guests ask to be shown to the toilet so they may wash their hands. The main course is served in and eaten from a large, common platter, and the couple choose morsels of food from wherever they can reach, trying to keep up polite conversation throughout the meal. Soon after the tea and cookies, they take their leave.

What did they do wrong? Almost everything. They confused their host by asking him to fix the hour, for in the Moslem world an invitation to a meal is really an invitation to come and spend time with your friends, during the course of which time, God willing, a meal may very well appear. To ask what time you should come is tantamount to asking your host how long he wants you around and implies, as well, that you are more interested in the meal than in his company.

One should be careful about asking after a Moslem man's wife; she frequently does not eat with foreign guests, even if female spouses are present, nor would she necessarily even be introduced. In any case, she belongs in the kitchen guaranteeing the meal is as good as she can produce, thereby showing respect for her guests and bringing honor on her and her husband's house. Nor should one praise the intelligence or good looks of small children, for this will alert evil spirits to the presence of a prized object in the home, and they may come and cause harm. It was not appropriate to ask to be shown the toilet either, for a decorative basin would have been offered for the washing of hands (and the nicer it is the more honor it conveys upon the family). Nor should one talk during the meal; it interferes with the enjoyment of the food to have to keep up a conversation and may even be interpreted as a slight against the cooking. And one should only take food from the part of the platter directly in front, not from anywhere within reach. Not only is it rude to reach, but doing so deprives the host of one of his chief duties and pleasures: finding the best pieces of chicken or lamb and ostentatiously placing them before the guest. Culture shock, clearly, is not just something we experience, it's something we inflict as well.

The potential of culture to confound and surprise us—and through us to surprise and confound others—is staggering. Our two lists, as any seasoned expatriate can attest, have barely scratched the surface. This is significant, for it is not simply— nor even principally—the *nature* of the experiences we have abroad that makes adjustment difficult, but rather the *scale*. Most of us are quite capable of handling an occasional encounter with unexpected, unfamiliar behavior; we do it all the time. It's the constant onslaught that takes some getting used to.

Let's conjure up a typical morning in the life of an expatriate development worker in Tunisia, and, to load the equation, let's make her a woman. She enjoys a quiet breakfast in the sanctity of her home and then begins the drive to work. The streets are thronged with pedestrians, choked with donkey carts, and full of aggressive Tunisian drivers who take regular and prolonged solace in their car horns. She is alternately immobilized by all the confusion and driven to fits of frightening recklessness. She stops briefly at the post office, long enough to be intimidated by the throng of men pressed around the stamp seller's window, and leaves without mailing her letters. At ten o'clock she reports for an appointment at the Ministry of Health and sits down to wait for the man she has come to see, assured by his secretary that he is due any minute. After forty-five minutes and several more assurances from the secretary, she leaves (and learns later that the man was out of town for the day and, further, knew that he would be when she pressed for the appointment). On her way back to her office she stops to buy the *International Herald Tribune* and have a cup of coffee. The paper isn't available, though the vendor assured her the day before it would be (God's will, he shrugs), and she is harassed by several male customers as she tries to relax with her coffee.

If we look closely at what transpires during just one of these incidents (they are all Type 1 in this case), we begin to understand what gives them their sting. Let's take the scene in the post office and imagine ourselves in the role of the development worker. We enter and locate the stamp window, but there's no line to stand in. Instead, there's a throng of people (nearly all men) pressed against the counter in a heaving semicircle. After some time we make out that the way to get served appears to be to push through the crowd until we're at the window. But we aren't altogether certain and, in any case, we're not used to doing this and feel reluctant. On the other hand, if we don't make an effort, we may never mail our letter.

Consider the feelings this incident provokes in us: to begin with there is a certain amount of confusion and helplessness before we figure out what is happening. Then follows a moment of fear when we see what is expected of us. This in turn gives way to feelings of anger or irritation at being forced to behave in a way we aren't used to and, as it happens, we don't particularly approve of. We are also likely to feel some embarrassment as we elbow our way into the crowd, hoping we have understood the system correctly. Underlying all these emotions is a deep and abiding sense of anxiety. As we have not really understood what is going on here, we can not be sure what will happen next or, therefore, know if we will be able to cope. We are fundamentally ill at ease. Moreover, there's the possibility, however remote, that we may never get to the front of the "line" and be able to mail our letter (and this thought only triggers further anger and anxiety).

In a brief period, no more than a minute or two, we've run through a rather impressive inventory of unpleasant feelings: confusion, helplessness, fear, anger, frustration, embarrassment, and anxiety. Even so, we would probably be able to cope with such an incident if it occurred in isolation, but when the post office encounter is just one of a string of such encounters in the same morning, and this continues day in and day out for weeks, the cumulative impact can be considerable.

And all the while, don't forget, we are busy committing untold dozens of Type II incidents. We don't know exactly when or how, of course, but we are; of that there can be no doubt. In other words, as we experience an ever-expanding number of incidents of cultural affront, the realization awakens within us, however subconsciously, that surely we must be the perpetrators of cultural effrontery as well. As we blunder through the day and the week, suspecting—and frequently achieving—the worst, we can't help feeling awkward, inadequate, even foolish. "Being a foreigner," Robert Kohls has observed, is a new and, at least for a time, uncomfortable, even threatening experience. It can produce a persistent sense of insecurity vibrating just below the threshold of consciousness—something like a long-term, low-grade infection, not seriously disruptive but annoyingly debilitating.[2]

The legacy of Type I and Type II incidents experienced repeatedly over a period of time is chronic—and at times acute—stress and anxiety. And when this stress and anxiety come on top of that provoked by being in a new job, a new community, and a new country—and note that these stresses, like Tunisians at the post office, don't wait their turn—it's no wonder the expatriate has the odd dark moment and occasional crisis of self-doubt. "I never told you," confesses a character in Paul Scott's *The Day of the Scorpion,*

> but there was a time—my second month in India last year—when if someone had offered me a passage home I'd have accepted like a shot. Goodness knows I loved being with you. But during that second month I had what I can only describe as a permanent sinking heart. I hated everything, hated it because I was afraid of it. It was all so alien.[3]

Stress and anxiety (to say nothing of a permanent sinking heart) are conditions the normal, healthy person tries to avoid, whether at home or abroad. It's only natural, therefore, that if we find our encounters with the local culture stressful and otherwise unpleasant, we will begin to pull back from it. And by withdrawing and isolating ourselves from the culture, we seriously undermine any possibility of meaningful adjustment; we can hardly adjust to that which we decline to experience.

If we were to construct a model of the process of adjustment, we might present the three steps we've described thus far as follows:

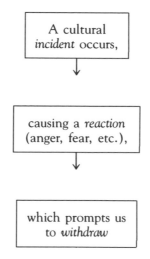

Figure I

In the case of a Type II incident, the sequence given above is the same, only it is we who are causing the incident and the local people who are withdrawing.

Successful cultural adjustment, as we shall see in succeeding chapters, consists of learning how to recognize and check this impulse to withdraw and, ultimately, how to transcend it. As it happens, Daphne Manners, Paul Scott's heroine quoted above, was not offered a "passage home," but many expatriates are. And they accept it "like a shot."

We should note that on this question the expatriate parts company with the tourist. Those same cultural incidents that are so many thorns in the sojourner's side are, of course, mere grist for the tourist's mill. Incidents, after all, make wonderful stories— and the best parts of travel books. They are one of the principal reasons travelers leave their home shores in the first place; they want what they encounter abroad to be strange, confusing, and even a little bit threatening. "Many visitors to Turkey," Philip Glazebrook writes, have been concerned to feel as strongly as possible the alienness of the place, not its familiarity. It is to feel the outlandishness of abroad that I leave home—to feel the full strength of its distinctive foreign character.[4]

"I never found my explanation for the tracks," Bruce Chatwin writes, in a similar vein, about some mysterious footprints he came across in the Himalayas. "But then you don't travel in order to find explanations. You travel in order to find things that defy explanation."[5]

Expatriates, who have also been travelers in their time, must guard against this sentiment. They are not—or should not be—collectors of the exotic or shocking, but seekers of understanding. The traveler may want the world and its people to remain remote and mysterious, but the sojourner must try to know them. If that removes some of the romance from going abroad, it also removes much of the suffering. "Mystery is delightful and exciting," Aldous Huxley noted,

> but it is foolish to admire it too highly. A thing is mysterious merely because it is unknown. But it is best to know what is knowable.[6]

REFERENCES

1. Paul Scott, *The Day of the Scorpion* (New York: Avon, 1979), 113.

2. L. Robert Kohls, *Survival Kit for Overseas Living*, 38.

3. Paul Scott, 114.

4. Philip Glazebrook, *Journey to Kars*, 183.

5. Bruce Chatwin, "An Unexpected Encounter in Nepal," *Esquire*, December 1983.

6. Aldous Huxley, *Along the Road* (Freeport, NY: Books for Libraries Press, 1971), 39.

■ 3 ■

A GOOD TIME

The British colony lived what appeared to be a life of blameless monotony, rolling about in small cars, drinking at the yacht club, sailing a bit, going to church, and suffering agonies of apprehension at the thought of not being invited to Government House on the Queen's birthday. One saw the murk creeping up over Brixton as one listened to their conversations. How often they have been described and how wearisome they are.

—LAWRENCE DURRELL
Bitter Lemons

There are children, frail and moribund, who live inside plastic bubbles; their immune systems have not developed, and so they have to be protected from the outside world, their air specially filtered, and their nourishment passed to them through special ducts, by gloved and sterile hands. Professional expatriates live like that. . . . They carry about with them the plastic bubble of their own culture, and nothing touches them until it has been filtered through the protective membrane of prejudice, the life-support system that forms their invisible excess baggage when they move on, from one contract to the next, to another country and another set of complaints.

—HILARY MANTEL
"Last Morning in Al Hamra"
Spectator 24 January 1987

As we have noted, many, perhaps most, people who live and work abroad are willing, even eager, to make the necessary effort to adjust to the local culture. And the great majority fail in the attempt. In this chapter we will examine where they go wrong, for it is precisely by being aware of and side-stepping the more common obstacles to successful adjustment that we stand the best chance of achieving it.

Why is it, then, that so many people with high hopes and quite the opposite intention end up cultural malcontents, or, in the case of those who go home, cultural casualties? The answer, simply put, is because it's so easy, even natural. It requires virtually no effort; it happens practically of its own accord and quite without our knowing about it. This is why it is so common.

What can be more normal, after all, than to shrink from unpleasant situations, to avoid that which we fear or dislike or find embarrassing? If we don't enjoy feeling irritated and confused at the post office or making fools of ourselves at the bazaar, then sooner or later we will contrive other ways to get our stamps and find someone else to do the marketing. This is nothing more than the instinctive human reaction of self-defense. As it happens, it is also the first step down the road to cultural maladjustment.

This becomes clearer when we consider what happens next. Because of the steady diet of embarrassing, frustrating, or otherwise unpleasant situations that are part of the experience of living overseas, particularly during the early months, what begins innocently enough as a reflex action toward self-protection quickly hardens into a pattern of systematic evasion and withdrawal. There then arises the insidious dynamic wherein the more we retreat from the culture and the people, the less we learn about them; the less we know about them, the more uncomfortable we feel among them; the more uncomfortable we feel among them, the more inclined we are to withdraw. The whole process happens without our knowing it; indeed, it happens *because* we are so unaware. While it may not be our conscious intention to isolate ourselves from the people and the culture, unconsciously this is precisely our goal, for in the end the people and the culture are inseparable from that very unpleasantness that is the source of our agitation.

Now the process of withdrawal begins to accelerate. In full flight from the indigenous culture, yet unwilling to pull up stakes and go home (those who aren't so unwilling will now do so), we seek a refuge, a society we can belong to and continue to function within. And the perfect one springs instantly to hand: the world of the expatriate subculture—also known as the foreign colony—the community of all those who have fled before us and fashioned for themselves a parallel culture, wherein they have achieved the rather dubious distinction of living abroad without ever leaving home. We will examine this society more closely in a moment, but for now suffice it to say that we are welcomed into this community with open arms and, if the truth be told, we are more than a little relieved to find ourselves under its protection. This, too, is only natural; confused and overwhelmed by all that is happening to us, we take comfort in being among people we understand and who instinctively understand us. It's exactly the same relief we feel when we spot someone we know in a roomful of strangers. Paul Scott writes:

> There was as well, India which at first seemed strange, even frightening . . . but [Daphne] was aware now of a sense of community. That sense sprang, she knew, from the seldom voiced, but always insistent . . . clan-gathering call to solidarity that was part of the social pattern she had noted early on and disapproved of. She still disapproved of it but she was honest enough to recognize it as having always been a bleak but real enough source of comfort and protection.[1]

For most sojourners, the safe harbor offered by the expatriate subculture, intended as no more than a place to catch one's breath, evolves quickly enough into a permanent home. It is a familiar, comfortable world; it beckons to us even as the alien world of the local culture seems to be pushing us away. And most of us succumb without a struggle.

The stage is now set for the next phase in the making of a cultural malcontent. Even as we slip comfortably into the expatriate lifestyle, our conscience is not clear. We sense, even if we can't put it into words, what we are about; we have undertaken to trivialize the experience of living abroad and to undermine our own professional effectiveness. For those of us who were sincere in our desire to confront and come to know another culture, or even just to succeed in our work, there can be no question but that we have compromised ourselves.

This is not a pleasant realization, particularly as it obliges us, if we are still taking ourselves seriously, to come clean, to eschew the comfortable niche we've begun to carve out in the expatriate colony and go forth once again to encounter the local culture. But there is a ready solution, such as it is: we can simply deny any responsibility for what has happened and shift the blame back onto the culture. It is not we who have withdrawn, we'll find ourselves saying (or at least thinking), but the culture which is closed or just too different for us to fathom. In any case, we rationalize, ours is an honorable retreat. Thus we can have our cake and eat it too: we continue to belong to the expatriate culture (and remain abroad) and at the same time feel little or no regret.

It's a pernicious process: the more intense our disappointment in ourselves, the more desperate the effort to blame and, in time, to indict the culture. The more we withdraw from the people, the more fault we find with them. The less we know about the culture, the more we seem to dislike it. And the worst of it is that in the end we begin to believe the very lies we've invented to console ourselves. As Kalvero Oberg has written:

> This hostility grows out of the genuine difficulty the visitor experiences in the process of adjustment. There is mail trouble, school trouble, language trouble, house trouble, transportation trouble, shopping trouble, and the fact that people in the host country are largely indifferent to all these troubles. [So] you band together with your fellow countrymen and criticize the host country, its ways and its people. . . . You take refuge in the colony of your countrymen and its cocktail circuit, which often becomes the fountainhead of emotionally charged . . . stereotypes.[2]

Life in the expatriate community tends to be sterile and vaguely unsatisfying. There is about it the aura of missed opportunities and a failure of the will. More often than not what binds its members together is not personal affinity or mutual respect or even common interests but a shared reluctance to delve into the local culture and take what comes. Members of the community haven't sought each other out so much as they have collided with each other in their common flight from the indigenous culture. The irony is that if they only took the time to find out, the expatriates might discover they share as many values and interests with the natives they have declined to befriend as with their compatriots with whom they force themselves to fraternize. Peopled with such strange and unwilling bedfellows, the expatriate community is in many respects not a true community at all. "There was my life in the hospital," Scott's heroine Daphne Manners observes,

> which also included the [all British] club and the boys and girls and all the good-time stuff that wasn't really good at all, just the easiest, the least exciting, so long as you ignored the fact that it was only the easiest for the least admirable part of your nature.

> After a while I began to see that the ease of companionship wasn't really ease at all, because once you had got to know each other, and had then to admit that none of you really had much in common except what circumstances had forced on you, the companionship seemed forced itself.[3]

The expatriate community, if it is to survive, must be worked at. It is, after all, something of an illusion, and illusions, as any actor can testify, require constant attention. So there are committees and committee meetings, cultural events, amateur theatricals, tennis tournaments, barbecues, fund drives, and, of course, charity events. Contact is imperative, though the quality of the contact is not nearly as important as the fact and frequency of it. The average expatriate, even if he or she had the inclination to make contact with the local people, hardly has the time for it. And after a while, the desire no longer arises. "Everyone in the ship menaces us with the prospect of a very good time in India," Aldous Huxley writes of his voyage to Asia in the 1920s,

> A good time means going to the races, playing bridge, drinking cocktails, dancing till four in the morning, and talking about nothing. And mean-

> while the beautiful, the incredible world [we've
> come to see] awaits our explorations, and life is
> short. . . . Heaven preserve me, in such a world,
> from having a Good Time! I shall see to it that my
> time in India is as bad as I can make it.[4]

For a veritable textbook illustration of cultural maladjustment in practice, we might look briefly at British colonial life in India during the period of the Raj, the ninety years between the famous mutiny of 1857 and the achievement of Indian independence in 1947. While the Raj may have been an extreme manifestation of cultural isolation and may also have exhibited features peculiar to the time, the place, and the two cultures involved, many of the attitudes and much of the behavior of the *sahibs* and *memsahibs* persist in expatriate communities today.

Rather than adapt, the British chose to construct uncannily accurate replicas of Wiltshire and Devon villages, complete with parade grounds, bandstands (with bands), stone churches, picket fences, gravel walkways, even golf courses where feasible, clinging tenaciously to a lifestyle more passionately British, if the truth be told, than many of them had ever lived back home.

"We were in India," an expatriate recalls in Charles Allen's *Plain Tales from the Raj,*

> we were looked after by Indian servants and we met
> a great many Indians, and some of us undoubtedly
> made a very close study of India and Indian cus-
> toms, but once you stepped inside the home you
> were back in Cheltenham or Bath. We brought with
> us in our home lives almost exact replicas of the sort
> of life that upper middleclass people lived in En-
> gland at that time. . . . You went from bungalow to
> bungalow and you found the same sort of furniture,
> the same sort of dinner table set, the same kind of
> conversation. We read the same books, mostly im-
> ported by post from England, and I can't really say
> that we took an awful lot from India.[5]

Nor is that so surprising, for as another of Allen's interviewees recalls:

> As far as possible the military cantonment was self-
> contained—with its own approved bazaar—and ac-

cess to the local community limited. The first order
that appeared when you got to a new station usually
stated that all Indian villages, Indian shops, Indian
bazaars and the civil lines were out of bounds to all
troops. (184)

But not only to the troops. "Our parents thought we'd catch
something if we went down to the bazaar," one woman remembers,

> But my brother and I always looked upon the bazaar
> as being too exciting. All those lovely stalls covered
> with sticky sweets and silver paper and piles of
> fruit. . . . I'll never forget the smell and all the heat
> and the movement and the people and the colour.
> There was a little temple which had rows and rows
> of little bells all round . . . and I remember think-
> ing, "Now that's marvelous! If only I could go past
> and jingle a few bells!" But no, the bazaar was a for-
> bidden land when I was a child. (27)

At the hub of this self-contained world was the Club, the exclusively British (in most cases, except, of course, for the servants) watering hole where the sahibs and memsahibs gathered
every day to play bridge or snooker, write letters, read back issues of the *Illustrated London News* or month-old copies of the
Times, gossip, plan a hunt (or a wedding), and speculate on
how soon before the rains might begin. "In any town in India,"
George Orwell wrote in *Burmese Days*, "the European Club is
the citadel, the real seat of the British power, the Nirvana for
which native officials and millionaires pine in vain." (116) "We
spent our time watching our step and watching what we said,"
another of Allen's oldtimers recalls,

> and there was a certain relief to go amongst people
> of our own race [at the club] and let our hair down.
> On almost any evening you would see the club ve-
> randah . . . occupied by literally hundreds of people
> in groups of two, four, and upwards. They would be
> busily chatting amongst themselves [and] drinks
> would be flowing freely. . . . Within those "basket
> chair circles" the conversation was said to be trivial
> in the extreme. A small community continually re-
> meeting could not be very original. (119, 124)

One could always decline to participate in the expatriate culture, of course, and go one's own way, but such independent types (generally written off as misfits or eccentrics) were not appreciated (as they are not today). Their independence had about it the air of disapproval (or was it superiority?), even criticism of the colonial subculture, and these nonconformists were accordingly regarded as a threat to the stability of the community:

> Some people refused to kowtow to all these social
> things and refused to belong to the Club. . . . [But]
> you were unwise not to become a club member if you
> could. If you didn't belong . . . you were an outcast,
> a rebel, a rather courageous rebel. (117)

"The other guests left this morning," writes J.R. Ackerley in *Hindoo Holiday*, his delightful account of his experiences in India in the 1920s as private tutor to a native prince,

> and just before starting Mrs. Montgomery gave me
> final advice. "You'll never understand the dark and
> tortuous minds of the natives," she said, "and if you
> do I shan't like you—you won't be healthy."[6]

Daphne Manners (in Paul Scott's *The Jewel in the Crown*) epitomized the "courageous rebel" and was subjected to the inevitable ostracism. "You English all felt that she didn't want you," one of Daphne's Indian friends declares, "want any of you, and of course among exiles that is a serious breach of faith. It amounts to treachery."[7]

Cultural withdrawal reached its supreme expression in the life of the memsahibs, the wives of the men of the civil and military services. Unlike their husbands, whose work brought them in contact with the native population, the women never needed to interact with India if they didn't wish to. While there are outstanding examples of British women who entered enthusiastically into the rhythms of Indian life, the majority of the memsahibs "lived a life more English than the English [and] more often than not the real India passed them by."[8] "One of these ladies," wrote a vistor to India in the 1850s,

> asked what she'd seen of the country and the people
> since coming to India, replied, "Oh, nothing thank

goodness. I know nothing at all about them. Nor do I wish to. Really I think the less one knows of them the better."[9]

With nothing to do and the whole day to do it in, the memsahibs whiled away their exile smoothing the rough edges and putting the finishing touches on what Geoffrey Moorhouse has called "India Britannica":

> Discouraged in the first place from making real contact with India and lacking the will to pick up more than a smattering of language adequate for speaking to the servants, the memsahibs became progressively more isolated . . . in a frigid expatriate subcommunity of their own. They were renowned for their attempts to reproduce English gardens, complete with lawns like green velvet, in tropical or semi-desert conditions that turned all vegetation either to dust or jungle within a few months. They were notable for imitating festive celebrations of home with dogged devotion, even if the Christmas dinner did consist of pea-fowl much more often than turkey. They waited eagerly for the arrival of catalogues from the big London stores, which reached India towards the end of summer . . . so that if you moved fast you might expect to order Christmas presents and receive them just in time.
>
> [Their] daily routine went something like this; up at 5 A.M. with horse-riding till 7 A.M.; breakfast on the verandah, followed by a cold bath before dressing to receive visitors at 10 A.M.; anything up to four hours of social chat with the visitors; lunch at 2 P.M. followed by a siesta, which might amount to lying in bed with a book till it was time to ride again and enjoy more social chat or a stroll near the bandstand, where the military musicians from the local garrison would play; after nightfall a supper party, with songs round the pianoforte until bedtime. This was a prescription for narrowing even further minds already constricted by the dominant attitudes of middle-class Victorian England. Few women would follow it unwaveringly day after day

> without becoming quite sure that they, and those
> like them, were naturally superior to the mass of
> humanity. [10]

Some observers even went so far as to blame the memsahibs

> for the break-up of relations between the British and
> the Indians. In the early days, before the English-
> woman went out to India at all, British officers spent
> much of their time with Indians, got to know them
> better, got to know the language well and so on;
> whereas once the Englishwoman started to arrive in
> India, she expected her husband to spend his time
> with her. She couldn't communicate with any-
> body . . . so she was forced to rely almost solely on
> her husband for amusement and company. [11]

In addition to the emotional and psychological consequences
of leading this lifestyle, their cultural obtuseness and insensitiv-
ity cost hundreds of British their lives and nearly cost England
control of much of northern India in the famous Mutiny of
1857. The incident which triggered the mutiny involved the is-
suing of a new kind of rifle to the army (in which only the
officers were British). While both the old and new rifles had to
be loaded through the muzzle, the cartridge of the new model
slipped in more smoothly if it was lubricated with a coating of
tallow, which was made from a compound of various animal
fats. When eighty-five orthodox Hindu and Moslem sepoys,
whose respective creeds forbade them to touch beef and pork
fat, refused to use the new rifles, they were stripped of their
uniforms, shackled, and sentenced to ten years in jail for insub-
ordination. "For Indians," Geoffrey Moorhouse observes,

> it was the penultimate humiliation. Next day, Sun-
> day, May 10, when officers and their families were
> getting ready for Evensong, fire broke out in the Na-
> tive Infantry Lines [in Meerut], then sepoys came
> running with guns, shooting at every European in
> sight. The long horror had begun. [But] the inci-
> dent . . . might have been avoided if British officers
> had been less obtuse; if they had not lost the habit
> of communicating with their men. [11]

Today, one hundred years after the heyday of the Raj, the
tradition of cultural isolation is alive and well in downtown

New Delhi. Americans have replaced the British as the most avid players, but the rules of the game—and the attitudes and behavior—remain essentially unchanged, as we can see in this 1986 *Washington Post* profile of life in the Foreign Service community in the Indian capital.

> New Delhi—In the heart of the unrelenting India of begging children and one-armed lepers, of hundreds of gods and streets of dust and 5,000 years of unfathomableness, lies a place that its inhabitants describe as an oasis of reason and order . . . what might be called "Americaland."

> Officially referred to as the U.S. Embassy compound, Americaland is nearly self-sufficient, spread over three adjacent complexes and 38 acres. It includes the embassy itself, the ambassador's residence, a school, a four-bed hospital, offices, apartments, a restaurant, a movie theater, a swimming pool, an athletic field, a bowling alley and a barbershop. The commissary sells Kraft mayonnaise, Purina Puppy Chow and Cheerios.

> Every time I leave the compound," says Al Friedbauer, a communications officer," "I feel like I'm going into a country I've never been to."

> In the second week of school, a special bus takes the high school Indian studies class on a tour of New Delhi. "Check it out—wow!" says Josh Langen, 16, as he looks out at a chaotic bazaar. He has moved to Delhi from Cairo three weeks before. "First time I've been out of the compound," he says. . . .

> "The biggest problem with any overseas school is trying to get the kids to give the culture a chance," admits Winthrop Sargent, the high school principal.

A few years ago some parents successfully pushed
for mandatory Indian studies . . . but even so,
teachers say it is the rare student who has the
time and the interest to dive into India.

For wives, the American Women's Association
organizes group expeditions into the old city of
Delhi to buy jewelry and go sightseeing. "A lot
of women don't feel comfortable going out, even
shopping, alone," says Diane Hughey, the
coordinator of the embassy's Community Liaison
Office.

Americaland seems to fulfill a certain need. It is
a study in how people grapple with culture shock.
It is not just that the phones don't work or the
electricity fails or that a boy comes to the door
with a sign that says he has no tongue and to
please give him money. The more difficult
problem is the isolation. Family and friends are
on the other side of the world, throwing people
back on their own resources. Doctors say that
while good marriages get better, bad marriages
become worse, and small problems can grow
beyond all reason into a crisis.

Judy Hansen, wife of a World Bank economist,
remembers bursting into tears when she couldn't
find an open drugstore to buy medicine for
strange, itching welts that had appeared on her
legs. It was June, 110 degrees. "I came back to
the house," she recalls, "and said: I just want to
go home. I can't take it anymore."

"I don't feel like I have any close Indian friends
[Hansen says in another context]. I really need to
make more of an effort. . . . " Susan and Al
Friedbauer feel the same way. "If I have a regret
in India," says Susan, a secretary at the embassy,
"it's that I haven't been able to make friends, just
to make friends. And that's sad. Because as much

as we like India, that would have enchanced our
appreciation of it." (*Washington Post*, 27
November 1986)

Many expatriates imagine they can have it both ways, that
they can live in another country and yet not be affected by—
nor themselves affect—the local people: "I leave them alone
and they leave me alone." The tactic here is not to deny the
reality of the indigenous culture but to deny that it need ever
have an impact on us. This might be possible if we could somehow contrive to live abroad and never come in contact with any
natives, but as contact is inevitable, there is bound to be an
impact, and that impact, in turn, produces a reaction. We can't
leave each other alone even if we want to. In the last analysis,
this denial of the impact of culture is just another kind of reaction, like frustration or agitation. It is not, as it seems to be, a
way of ducking the question of adjustment; it is merely a subtler
form of maladjustment.

In this same regard, we should remind ourselves that to be
ignorant (of another culture) does not mean we won't still feel
threatened by it. The unknown is inherently unsettling; we can
never be sure but that one day what we don't know will indeed
hurt us. To be ignorant of a foreign culture is, in the end, to
fear—and therefore dislike—it.

It is important, as we noted in chapter 1, not to confuse
feeling at ease in an overseas setting with true cultural adjustment. The habitues of the foreign colony are no doubt su-
premely comfortable in their cultural bubble and they are
unquestionably overseas, but we can't honestly say that they
have come to terms with the local culture. Theirs is plainly a
response to the culture, but we can hardly call it an adjustment.

At the same time we should note that while we have been
critical of the expatriate subculture in these pages, for some sojourners it is a legitimate, even honorable, refuge. Not everyone
who goes abroad is capable of adjusting to the local culture.
Moreover, those who may adapt readily enough to one culture
may not adapt at all to another. For those individuals, making a
life for themselves in the foreign colony often represents a con-

siderable accomplishment. They will want, however, to beware of some of the more unwholesome behaviors that can be found in the foreign colony—in particular the tendency to disparage the natives—and look for every opportunity to learn more about the local culture.

None of what we have said is to suggest that the sojourner who wishes to adapt overseas must forego the company of other expatriates. This would be unnatural; to ignore the reality of one's own cultural identity is just as nonsensical as ignoring that of the local people. Moreover, a case can be made that a certain degree of what we might call strategic cultural withdrawal is entirely appropriate, even healthy, especially during the early weeks in-country when the impact of being abroad is most intense. As long as we don't shrink from further contact, there's nothing wrong with retreating from time to time to recharge our batteries.

But we must be careful lest we begin trusting our instincts entirely in this matter, for they will invariably draw us deeper into the expatriate web, and before we know it, a little innocent contact with fellow sojourners has become an exclusive way of life. In the end, the time and effort spent befriending other sojourners must necessarily come at the expense of reaching out to the local culture.

All the while we should keep in mind that our reaction to the local culture does not go unnoticed by its inhabitants; indeed, it often provokes a counter-reaction of its own. The local people are aware of our behavior, and they can't help noticing that we seem to keep our distance and socialize largely with other expatriates. They note—and they begin to accommodate—our preferences. Even as we withdraw from them, they become less inclined to seek us out. Thus, the gap between cultures widens from both sides simultaneously and becomes all the more formidable.

"It would be better if they went to church," an Eskimo says of the development workers who live with the natives in Canada's far north,

> even if they could not understand. It would show
> that they had some interest in what is happening in
> the settlement. Perhaps some problems would not
> arise if the Whites bothered to go to church with

the Eskimos; maybe they would understand things better. It would make the people think that the Whites *belong* to the settlement.[13]

No one who goes abroad can avoid the kind of cultural incidents described in chapter 2, and these incidents, in turn, invariably trigger our instinct to escape from uncomfortable situations. And we begin to withdraw. It all happens without our knowing it, when we aren't looking. Or, more accurately, it happens *because* we aren't looking, because we aren't aware of our own behavior.

But this process is not inevitable; we do not have to withdraw from situations we find unpleasant. Or, rather, we can train ourselves not to. And in so doing, as we shall see in chapter 5, we take the first and most crucial step down the road to successful cultural adjustment.

But we are getting ahead of ourselves. It's time now to return to the scene of cultural contact, to the Tunisian post office where the throng of men is still pressed against the stamp seller's window and we are still standing there off to one side, perplexed and on the verge of annoyance.

REFERENCES

1. Paul Scott, *The Jewel in the Crown*, 15.

2. Kalvero Oberg, "Culture Shock and the Problem of Adjusting to New Cultural Environments." As quoted in Pierre Casse, *Training for the Cross-Cultural Mind* (Washington, DC: SIETAR, 1981), 23.

3. Paul Scott, 385, 404.

4. Aldous Huxley, *Jesting Pilate* (London: Triad/Paladin, 1985), 11.

5. Charles Allen, *Plain Tales from the Raj* (London: Futura, 1984), 82.

6. J. R. Ackerley, *Hindoo Holiday* (New York: Penguin, 1983), 23–24.

7. Paul Scott, *The Day of the Scorpion*, 202.

8. Charles Allen, 213–14.

9. Christopher Hibbert, *The Great Mutiny: India 1857* (New York: Penguin, 1982), 37.

10. Geoffrey Moorhouse, *India Britannica* (London: Paladin, 1984), 94–95.

11. Christopher Hibbert, *The Great Mutiny: India 1857* (New York: Penguin, 1982), 37.

12. Geoffrey Moorhouse, 85–86.

13. Hugh Brody, *The People's Land* (New York: Penguin, 1975), 170.

■ 4 ■

THE WHOLE
LIVING SELF

The first thing an Englishman does on going
abroad is to find fault with what is French,
because it is not English.

—WILLIAM HAZLITT
Notes of a Journey Through France and Italy.

We come back, then, to the Bureau de Poste in Tunisia and to
that moment when, whether we realize it or not, we've encountered another culture. What we do next is crucial, for it is here,
at the precise moment we come in contact with culture, that
the process of adjustment must begin. In this chapter we will
examine what transpires at this critical juncture, why it happens, and what to do about it.

As we stand to one side, trying to make sense out of the
scene around the stamp seller's window, a feeling of uneasiness
comes over us. We don't understand what is happening or what
we ought to do next. Unsure what to do and increasingly anxious to do *something,* we become agitated. As we saw in chapter
3, it is to avoid just this kind of agitation that we pull back from
the culture around us and thereby set in motion the process of
withdrawal.

But why should this be? Why should there be anything unsettling about a group of people who, as it happens, don't line
up for their stamps? In fact, there isn't, that is, *it isn't the behavior itself that troubles us but the fact that we aren't expecting it,*
particularly not here in a post office. In its *proper* place—on a
subway platform, at the entrance to an amusement park or a

rock concert, waiting for a department store to open for its Memorial Day sale—we expect and know how to respond to a jostling, unruly crowd. But this isn't how people who buy stamps behave. Or, to be more precise, it isn't how *we* behave when we are buying stamps.

What we are witnessing here is one of the most fundamental truths of human behavior: namely, *each of us expects that everyone else is just like us. We expect everyone to behave as we do (the source of Type I incidents), and we assume we behave like everyone else (the source of Type II incidents).* This is true of our behavior as individuals and especially as members of a culture. "Deep down," Robert Kohls observes, "we assume that under normal circumstances we all think about and perceive the world in basically the same way."[1]

This assumption, which we are rarely, if ever, aware of, is the foundation and operative principle of much of human behavior. Indeed, if all of us did not live by this conviction, most human interaction would not be possible. Not surprisingly, it is at the heart of the problem of cross-cultural adjustment. If we turn again to the incidents presented in chapter 2, we will find this assumption lurking behind every one of them. As we aren't prone to urinate in the street, we are shocked when the Japanese do. We don't stare and we don't appreciate being stared at. We wouldn't dream of eating with our hands, hawking or breaking wind in public, or slurping our soup and we can't imagine others doing so. We speak to the point and expect everyone—the Japanese included—to do so as well. In each of these Type I examples, an incident has occurred because our assumption that everyone is like us has suddenly been challenged.

The same holds for Type II incidents. We aren't offended by our behavior, so how could others be? We don't regard it as offensive to walk between two people on opposite sides of the street without bowing and asking permission; why would they? We don't think it's rude not to belch after taking a drink (quite the contrary), and we can't imagine others would. We aren't offended by exposed arms and legs in public. We *like* it when people compliment our children. People are the same everywhere, aren't they?

Returning to our graphic model of the process of adjustment, we can now add a key new element at the beginning:

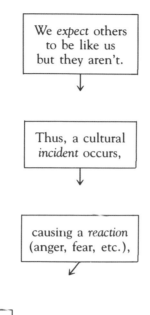

Figure 2.

If the cause of our problems is our instinctive assumption that everyone is like us, then, clearly, the solution must be to somehow eradicate this assumption, to pry loose its grip on our behavior. And this is, indeed, our goal, but to do this—and to appreciate the magnitude of the task—we first need to examine how we come by this assumption and how exactly it influences our behavior.

The first point we can make about this conviction is that we come by it quite naturally, that it is, in fact, inescapable. We assume others are like us for the simple reason that we learned how to behave by watching and imitating them. This is the process of conditioning through which we learn how to function in the world: by observing, imitating (for which we are rewarded), and eventually internalizing the behavior of those around us. Up to the moment we go abroad—or otherwise have a significant encounter with people from another culture or subculture—we have no reason or basis for believing that other people, *including foreigners*, might behave differently—for believing, in other words, that some of the behavior we've picked up over the years might be peculiar to our particular group or society. Even if we suspect as much, we cannot conceive of what the behavior of foreigners might be like. We cannot expect a Tunisian to behave like a Tunisian if we've never met a Tunisian. We are obliged by the limits of our experience to expect a Tunisian to behave the way all the other people we know have always behaved: like us. Thus, while we may not choose to assume that others are like us, while we may even *know* better than to assume that others are like us, and while we may very much wish we could stop expecting everyone to be like us, the force of our conditioning leaves us no alternative.

Let's take an example: Nearly everyone is familiar with the scene in the film *Star Wars* where Luke Skywalker and Obiwan Kenobe, in search of an experienced pilot, go into a bar crowded with an astonishing assortment of extraterrestrial customers. While the makers of the film were able to design a number of nonhuman creatures for this scene, they were at a loss to come up with any correspondingly nonhuman behavior. Indeed, this is precisely what gives this scene its impact: the sight of creatures so bizarre behaving just like the boys at your neighborhood watering hole. This same conceit animates Stephen Spielberg's film *E.T.*: the little fellow may look rather odd, but underneath he's just like you and me. In fact—and this is the point—he *has* to be, for neither you nor I (nor Stephen Spielberg) can conceive of nonhuman behavior; there are no models. We even conceive of animals in human terms, explaining their behavior in reference to our own.

The same applies to the question of culture; someone from Georgia or Wisconsin cannot imagine how an Ecuadorian might feel or act. We are obliged to imagine Ecuadorians feeling and acting—not to mention thinking—much as we do ourselves. And vice versa. "It is impossible," Philip Glazebrook writes, "to guess what responses to a given set of circumstances or surroundings may be going through the head of someone from the other side of the world."[2]

"When you meet a Gethenian," observes the narrator of Ursula Le Guin's science fiction classic *The Left Hand of Darkness* (see appendix 2),

> you cannot and must not do what a bisexual naturally does, which is to cast him in the role of Man or Woman, while adopting towards him a corresponding role dependent on your expectations of . . . persons of the same or opposite sex. Our entire pattern of socio-sexual interaction is non-existent here. They cannot play the game. They do not see one another as men or women. *This is almost impossible for our imagination to accept.*[3] (Italics added.)

The old proverb notwithstanding, we cannot put ourselves in someone else's shoes. Or, rather, we can, but it's still our own feet we will feel.

Another point about our conditioning is that it operates subconsciously; we are not aware that we harbor these innumerable expectations about how people are going to behave. We don't go into the post office thinking: "Now I am expecting a line" or "Now I am expecting the man behind the window to have stamps, be civil, have two eyes, give the corrrect change, etc." William Weeks, et. al., wrote "Most of the influences that shape the interpersonal interaction patterns of an individual are unknown to him, and the patterns themselves are largely out of awareness."[4] It is only when our assumptions are confounded, when the postmaster wears an eyepatch or is out of stamps, that their presence, in the form of our shock or surprise, is briefly betrayed. But, as Edward Hall points out, to little avail:

> Most of culture lies hidden and is outside voluntary control, making up the warp and weft of human existence. It penetrates to the roots of [an individual's] nervous system and determines how he perceives the world. Even when small fragments of culture are elevated to awareness, they are difficult to change.[5]

And needless to say, behavior of which we are not aware is behavior that is difficult, if not impossible, to control.

We may not choose to be conditioned or have any control over our conditioning, but we should nevertheless be grateful for it; for without it we would not be able to function. If we were incapable of learning from our experience or of generalizing from past patterns of behavior, the world would be a hopelessly unpredictable, bewildering place. If we were not instinctively sure that people would be civil unless provoked, stay on their side of the road and stop on red, that shopkeepers would give us goods in return for money—if we could not routinely depend on these things happening—the resulting uncertainty would immobilize us. "Staying comfortable," Hall writes,

> is largely a matter of culture. Informal or core culture is the foundation on which interpersonal relations rest. All of the little things that people take for granted . . . depend on sharing informal patterns.[6]

Thus it is that the same conditioning that makes it so difficult for us to function overseas is what makes it possible for us to function at home.

Like most behavior, the assumption that everyone else is like us is learned; it is the product of our conditioning, of our coming in contact with the world around us. The difficulty, of course, is that the world of human interaction is partly shaped by culture and to that extent is not the same from country to country. What our world teaches us about how people behave is not the same as what the world of the Thais teaches them. Yet we each learn our respective lessons well.

But there's something wrong here, isn't there? In this age of the shrinking planet and the global village, we all know the world is composed of an enormous variety of peoples and that their beliefs and practices differ from our own in every conceivable manner. Cultural diversity is a truism, even a cliche, of our time. Indeed, it is precisely to satisfy our curiosity in this regard that so many of us go abroad in the first place. How is it possible, then, to be steeped in the notion of cultural diversity and at the same time assume everyone else is just like us? Surely the one precludes the other.

Not necessarily. What we know to be true (or right or best) is not always what drives our actions. What the conscious intellect knows (in this case, that other people are *not* like us) is often no match for what a lifetime of conditioning has taught us. For the notion of cultural diversity to take deep and lasting root in our psyche, it must be reinforced over a sustained period, like any notion that aspires to one day become a conditioned reflex. Until that time, it's quite possible for us to cheerfully subscribe to the view that all people are different and still be stunned to come across a Hindu drinking cow urine.

"Like most people who have never traveled abroad," Sinclair Lewis writes of his hero in *Dodsworth*,

> Sam had not *emotionally* believed that these foreign scenes veritably existed; that human beings could really live in environments so different from the front yards of Zenith suburbs; that Europe was anything save a fetching myth.[7] (Italics added.)

To put it another way, what we have actually experienced, what we know to be real, will always have more truth for us—more hold over our actions—than what we've only read or heard about. Moreover, what we've experienced repeatedly will affect us much more than what we've experienced only once or twice. "Of the fact that it takes all sorts to make a world I have been aware ever since I could read," Aldous Huxley writes,

> But proverbs are always platitudes until you have experienced the truth of them. The newly arrested thief knows that honesty is the best policy with an intensity of conviction which the rest of us can never experience. And to realize that it takes all sorts to make a world one must have seen a certain number of the sorts with one's own eyes.
>
> There is all the difference in the world between believing academically, with the intellect, and believing personally, intimately, with the whole living self.[8]

This is a crucial distinction; many sojourners and would-be sojourners confuse a passing familiarity with the notion of cultural diversity, a mere acceptance of the fact that different people behave differently, with the ability to adjust to another culture, or, in some cases, with the actual *achievement* of adjustment.

This becomes all the more significant when we remember that many sojourners are at great pains to educate themselves about the country they are going to. They read all they can find about it and talk to others who have lived there. It is even likely, these days, that they will participate in some kind of training or orientation sponsored by their company or organization and designed and executed by specialists in the field of intercultural communication. Quite naturally, these sojourners (and their sponsors) assume that this program has prepared them for the experience just ahead and that if it hasn't taken the shock out of culture shock altogether, it has at least mitigated the lion's share. When they discover that it hasn't (for the reasons given above), when the unpleasantness and stress all expatriates are prey to become evident, the prepared and oriented sojourners are all the more vulnerable for having had their expectations raised and their confidence inflated.

Conditioning—our experience of the world—is at the heart of the problem of crossing cultures. As it happens, it is likewise at the heart of the solution: just as we learn, through experience, to expect everyone to behave as we do, so we can also learn—through experience—to expect certain people to behave differently. The trick, as we shall see in the next chapter, is to allow ourselves to *have* the experiences that will bring about this change in our expectations.

REFERENCES

1. L. Robert Kohls, *Survival Kit for Overseas Living*, 56.

2. Philip Glazebrook, *Journey to Kars*, 40.

3. Ursula K. Le Guin, *The Left Hand of Darkness* (New York: Ace Books, 1977), 94.

4. William Weeks, Paul Pedersen, and Richard Brislin, *A Manual of Structured Experiences for Cross-Cultural Learning* (Yarmouth, Maine: Intercultural Press, 1977), xv.

5. Edward T. Hall, *The Hidden Dimension* (New York: Anchor Books, 1969), 188.

6. Edward T. Hall, *The Dance of Life* (New York: Anchor Press/ Doubleday, 1984), 195.

7. Sinclair Lewis, *Dodsworth,* excerpted in Paul Fussell, ed., *The Norton Book of Travel* (New York: W.W. Norton, 1987), 691.

8. Aldous Huxley, *Jesting Pilate,* 207.

■ 5 ■

THE ORGAN OF BELIEF

"Take it easy darling," he would say. "We've got to be absorbed into these customs. We're still too tough to be ingested quickly, but we've go to try and soften ourselves. We've got to yield."

—ANTHONY BURGESS
The Enemy in the Blanket

The born traveller—the man who is without prejudices, who sets out wanting to learn rather than to criticize, who is stimulated by oddity, who recognizes that every man is his brother, however strange and ludicrous he may be in dress and appearance—has always been comparatively rare.

—HUGH AND PAULINE MASSINGHAM
The Englishman Abroad

It might be useful to review what we've discovered thus far about the process of cultural adjustment. We began by noting that, in fact, it is not to culture per se that one must adapt, but to culture as manifest and encountered in the behavior of individual foreigners. We then observed that, strictly speaking, it isn't even the actions of foreigners that put us off—most behavior is essentially neutral—but the fact that we aren't expecting particular behaviors in particular situations, and, as a result, we don't know how to respond. The reason we aren't expecting the behaviors that so confound us is that our conditioning—the sum of our experiences of the world—has taught us (as it teaches people everywhere) that everyone behaves more or less as we do. We not only assume this to be true, we depend on its being true. When we go abroad and discover it is not, we aren't merely surprised, we are also threatened. The resulting agitation provokes us to withdraw from and avoid the culture around us. Some sojourners, as we've noted, withdraw definitively and return home; others remain abroad but withdraw instead into themselves and the expatriate subculture, in the manner and with the consequences we chronicled in chapter 3. Neither group can be said to have adapted successfully to living overseas.

Before taking up the solution to the problem, we should expand briefly on one of the statements made above. It is not, we have said, the behavior of foreigners that puts us off, but the fact that we aren't accustomed to certain actions in certain settings and don't quite know what to do. The problem is the difference in behavior, to which each side contributes equally. But the burden of the solution must inevitably lie with the visitor. We can't expect Tunisians to change their behavior to suit our expectations, so it is up to us to change our expectations to conform to Tunisian behavior. We are the ones, after all, who have gone abroad; as guests we can't very well demand that our hosts adjust to us.

Any solution to the problem of adjustment must come into play precisely at those moments when we actually encounter culture, as it were, in the flesh: when we feel ourselves becoming agitated in the post office in Tunisia, when we are shocked at the sight of Afghans eating with their hands, when we are disgusted by the hawking and spitting of Indians or irritated by the indirectness of the Japanese. It is here, in the grip of these emotions, that we begin to develop those feelings of aversion for the local people which, if unchecked, lead soon enough to that pattern of avoidance and withdrawal. But if these feelings could somehow be controlled and neutralized, if we could somehow intervene in these moments of cultural discomfort, then all they give rise to would never come to pass.

The trick is to train ourselves to become aware of these feelings *as they arise* and identify them immediately for what they are. If we are aware that we are feeling disgust or agitation at the moment these feelings come over us and if we reflect on why we are experiencing those emotions—because something we depend on happening, something we require to happen, does not—if we do these two things at the moment of cultural truth, then the feelings of disgust and agitation will of their own accord—and of necessity—dissipate.

Why? In the first place, the very act of being aware of our anger or disgust will cause it to abate somewhat, for we cannot be aware of what is causing our anger and simultaneously experience the anger itself. The mind cannot hold two objects at once, though the mind works so fast it may seem that it can. So long as our attention is diverted from whatever is making us angry, for that period (however brief) the emotion, cut off from its object, is checked. It is likely to return, of course, as soon as our awareness lapses (or another object comes along), but so long as our awareness is sustained, the anger cannot intrude into our consciousness.

Similarly, when we reflect on the reason for our anger, which we can only do after we have dispelled the anger itself, and realize that we have become agitated not because of something the Tunisians have done to us but because of what we, by expecting them to be like us, have done to ourselves, then the power of this realization neutralizes much of our frustration. If we can allow this reflection and realization to occur, then our agitation is bound to subside. If it does not, then it's because we choose to indulge it (although in some instances, as we shall see later in this chapter, the behavior in question is so offensive that even awareness cannot completely mitigate our reaction).

With our reactions to cultural incidents thus muted (we are only talking about Type I incidents for the moment), the way is clear for the next step in the process. As our anger (or shock or agitation) begins to subside, we are then—*and only then*—in a position to observe what is going on around us, to truly *experience* the situation in which we find ourselves. Just as we cannot simultaneously be angry and be aware of our anger, neither can we be angry and at the same time take in what is happening in the post office. *We cannot experience and react to a situation simultaneously.* We can have an experience of anger or we can have an experience of the post office, but we can't have both. Thus it is that in becoming aware of and thereby muting our anger, we permit ourselves to experience the Tunisian post office.

And if we can do that, we can adjust to another culture.

Let's go back to the post office and see what we would experience if we only allowed ourselves to. There is the same crowd around the window, but as our agitation begins to subside, we may notice some or all of the following: that it is a relatively quiet and good-natured crowd, that other people entering the post office are not put off by the throng but immediately join it, that there may be some elbowing and jostling but no one seems offended by it, that the clerk is not particularly ruffled or anxious, that people in the middle or even at the back of the crowd seem to have the clerk's attention from time to time, that the clerk seems to be attending to several customers simultaneously, that people periodically leave the scene and appear to be satisfied. You will pick up more, of course, if you speak the local language and understand what is being said.

Whatever you manage to see—and there is a lot you won't be able to see in the beginning—will make an impression on you, and these impressions in turn form the basis of what you will expect the next time you go to the post office. Each time you will see more, and the more you see, the more accurate your expectations will be on each subsequent visit. It is a benign circle: the less you react, the more you see; the more you see, the more accurate your expectations; the more accurate your expectations, the less cause you will have to react. And the key to it all, to not reacting, is awareness.

Our goal, then, must be to create those interludes wherein, momentarily free of our subjective reactions, we can truly observe what is going on around us. What we thus observe becomes what we then expect when we go back to the post office. And to the extent those observations are correct, our expectations will accordingly be fulfilled: we will expect what in fact occurs. And as a consequence, there will be no surprises, no agitation, no basis to react. There will, in short, be no more incidents (at least not at the post office!).

"To have your eyes widened and your organ of belief stretched," Philip Glazebrook writes,

> whilst remaining discreetly submissive, seems to me
> a faculty the tourist ought to cultivate. . . . When

> you have submitted to looking about you discreetly
> and to observing with as little prejudice as possible,
> then you are in a proper state of mind to walk about
> and learn from what you see.[1]

Just as these unprejudiced observations are the key to adjustment, awareness is the key to these observations. They can only occur once our reactions (our prejudices) have been controlled, and our reactions can only be controlled when—and largely because—we become aware of them.

Returning to our graphic model of the process of adjustment, we can now complete it.

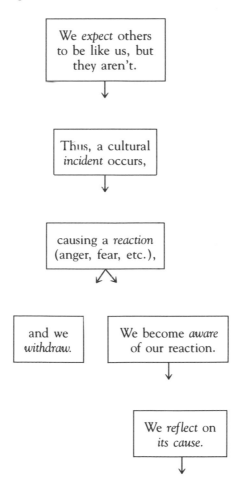

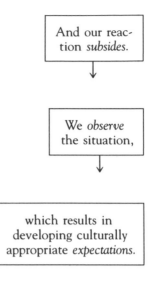

Figure 3

This is all well and good, you may be saying, but how exactly does one come by this elusive awareness? What can one do to develop and perfect it? Before tackling this question, we should first point out that the habit of awareness, by which we mean the instantaneous recognition of emotional states, runs counter to a lifetime of conditioning and instinct. It is our wont to *have* feelings, not to observe or control them; to be subject *to* our feelings, not to subject them to something else. All of which is not to say that awareness is beyond our reach, but only that it does not come without a struggle.

The first step, which we've already accomplished, is to gain an intellectual appreciation of the dynamic we've presented in these pages, to understand and accept —if only in principle— the notion that each of us expects other people to think, feel, and behave exactly as we do, and that, as a consequence, when we go abroad we often behave and react to the behavior of others inappropriately.

Once we have been exposed to and understand this truth in theory, we must then discover it at work in ourselves. This is the second step in developing awareness. And it is the most crucial, for unless we can be convinced that we actually behave in a particular manner, we will never be prompted to alter that behavior.

In the beginning we won't be aware of our expectations at the moment they arise (for if we were, that would constitute the very awareness we are trying to cultivate). Rather, we shall have to settle for and practice a kind of retrospective awareness, taking time at lunch or at the end of the day (but no later) and deliberately trying to recall moments when we were agitated or frustrated by something a local person said or did and then reflecting on why we reacted. In just this manner, by disciplining ourselves to recollect cultural incidents that have so far gone unremarked, we come face to face with the truth of our own behavior; we discover that we do indeed expect others to be like us. We look on (if only after the fact) as our expectations repeatedly trip us up and provoke those feelings of helplessness and irritation that lead us down the road to withdrawal.

It is a sobering sight, even in retrospect. But this is as it should be, for it is precisely the shock of seeing ourselves completely at the mercy of our conditioning, with our best intentions utterly thwarted, that gives us the jolt we need to act. Moreover, the practice of retrospective awareness, by instilling in us the habit of recollecting our emotional states, leads us in time, and without the need of any additional technique, to the threshold of simultaneous awareness (of our emotions), which is our goal. Retrospective awareness, in other words, not only shocks us into striving for true awareness, it is itself the means to that very end.

In a moment we will consider how to manage Type II incidents, but first we need to take up another category of Type I incident. Awareness, we have said, clears the way for objective observation which in turn teaches us culturally correct expectations. And thus does the bottom fall out of the whole avoidance/withdrawal syndrome. There are certain cases, however, as most expatriates are painfully aware, where mere observation—knowing what to expect—is not, by itself, sufficient to keep us from being put off by what we see. There are some behaviors, in other words, that will continue to provoke us even *after* we have conditioned ourselves to expect them.

Observation is effective—and usually sufficient—in those cases (the vast majority) where the behavior we encounter is essentially neutral, without moral or ethical dimensions, such as our example of the post office or of Germans working behind closed office doors or even of Afghans eating with their hands. We react in these instances not because our sense of right and wrong has been offended, but because we don't understand what is happening; we are confused, embarrassed, and anxious.

But there is another category of Type I incident wherein we expect precisely what in fact transpires, but we simply do not approve. In these cases we react not because we have been caught off our guard but because, to all appearances and so far as we can tell, a certain value we hold has been violated or ignored. As a consequence we feel angry, shocked, even disgusted. While observation can prepare us to *expect* these behaviors, it can hardly make us *like*—much less *adopt*—them. In these instances, only *observation coupled with understanding* can prevent us from being offended (and then not always, as we shall see).

Let's return to another incident from the day of our luckless female expatriate in Tunisia: the encounter at the newsstand. In this scene our sojourner gets upset when the news vendor fails to produce the *Herald Tribune* he "promised" the previous day. If this behavior persists, before very long our friend will pick up on this man's apparent disregard for the truth and stop believing him. Not expecting him to be as good as his word, she will no longer be surprised when he isn't. According to our technique of awareness, our friend has done everything "right" and ought, therefore, to feel "adjusted." But this isn't likely; rather, she probably feels put off by this fellow and may very well stop visiting his newsstand. In a word, she withdraws.

But consider how she might feel if she understood what the vendor—let's call him Abdullah— means when he says he will have the *Herald Tribune* on the morrow. Being a good Moslem, Abdullah instinctively adds the phrase *N'sha'llah* (God willing) to his statement, thereby clearly signaling (to other good Moslems, at any rate) the fact that he doesn't know or may even doubt there will be a paper the next day but that it is not for him to say what may or may not transpire concerning matters in the future. God (in whose domain the future squarely falls) may

contrive to put a *Herald Tribune* on the morning truck—
He's done stranger things than that before—and so long as this
remains a possibility, Abdullah would be presumptuous (not
to mention culturally insensitive) to suggest otherwise. In
short, when Abdullah says "Yes, N'sha'llah," what he means
is "no."

Knowing all this, which is clearly more than mere observation can teach her, will very likely temper our sojourner's reaction to Abdallah and cause her to judge him less harshly. She
may even continue to give him her business. At the very least,
she will be less inclined to avoid him.

In some cases, then, observation must be reinforced by specific cultural knowledge before we can accept or adjust to certain behavior. This is an important point, for we have said
rather emphatically that simply reading or hearing about another culture cannot prepare us for the experience of actually
encountering it. And so it cannot. Knowledge or cultural information cannot keep us from reacting to the natives—such is the
power of our conditioning—but it can help prevent us from judging them inappropriately, and this in turn can be a supporting
factor in our progress toward successful adjustment.

We should not take this to mean that awareness has no place
in these kinds of incidents. On the contrary, it is crucial, a necessary—if not sufficient—ingredient, for as we become aware of
anger or disgust arising within us, we must at that moment remind ourselves that we have just made a judgment and that we
may not know enough about the culture yet to have done so.
Or, to put it another way, we must remind ourselves that we
have made a judgment and that such a judgment is almost certainly based on our experience of our own culture and can only
be coincidentally of any use here in Tunisia. In any case, this
realization, coupled with the moderating influence of our having shifted our attention to our feelings and away from their object (the offending behavior), will take the sting out of our
reaction and prompt us to suspend our judgment. With the impact of the incident thus defused, we can then look for (or make
a note to look for) an explanation for the offensive behavior.

And even then we may not always find an explanation, or at
least one that satisfies us. That is, in every culture there will be
behaviors we cannot accept even after we have conditioned our-

selves to expect them *and after we have uncovered the cultural explanation behind them.* These behaviors will vary from individual to individual, but their defining characteristic is always the same: they violate values so fundamental to our identity that our continued self-respect demands we reject them.

In the case of Abdullah, when our friend understood why he acted the way he did, she was able to accept his behavior. She misunderstood, but in the end she did not disapprove, for there was not, as it turns out, anything offensive or unacceptable *behind* Abdullah's actions. But there will be other cases where even when she understands why the natives are behaving the way they are, she will be unable to accept the explanation. Or, more precisely, she will be able to accept that the explanation is valid for them, but she will never accept it as valid for her.

We might cite the incident in the cafe as a case in point. After her frustrating and stressful morning, our friend retires to a cafe to have a cup of coffee and relax, only to be harassed by the male customers present. By practicing awareness and observation she begins to notice that the men treat every woman in sight in the same manner, that few of these women pay much attention or seem annoyed, that none of the women passing by stop for a drink, and that she is in fact the only woman in the cafe. She concludes, on that or a subsequent visit, that women don't go alone to public places in Tunisia (at least not to cafes) and modifies her behavior accordingly (or does not change her behavior but now *expects* to be harassed in cafes). Once again, she has done everything "right," but chances are this doesn't make her feel any better. She still resents this aspect of the culture and may very well want nothing more to do with it.

Now let's assume she uncovers the explanation behind the offending behavior, that she picks up the requisite cultural knowledge (summarized in this passage from Fatima Mernissi's *Beyond the Veil*):

> Moslem sexuality is a territorial one, i.e., a sexuality whose regulatory mechanisms consist primarily of a strict allocation of space to each sex and an elaborate ritual for resolving the contradictions arising from the inevitable interferences between spaces. Apart from the ritualized trespasses of women into public spaces which are, by definition, male spaces,

there are no accepted patterns for interactions between unrelated men and women. . . .

Women using public spaces, trespassing on the male
universe, are restricted to few occasions and bound
by specific rituals such as the wearing of the
veil. . . . The veil means that the woman is present
in the men's world, but invisible; she has no right to
be in the street.

Women in male spaces are considered provocative
and offensive. If [a woman] enters [a male space],
she is upsetting the male's order and his peace of
mind. She is actually committing an act of aggres-
sion against him merely by being present where she
should not be. If the woman is unveiled, the situation is aggravated.

The male's response to the woman's presence is, according to the prevailing ideology, a logical response
to an exhibitionistic assault. It consists of pursuing
the woman for hours, pinching her if the occasion is
propitious, eventually assaulting her verbally; all in
the hope of convincing her to carry out her exhibitionistic propositioning to its implied end.[7]

While some sojourners may find this explanation acceptable
and no longer react to examples of this behavior, others will not
respond positively and will go on resenting the culture that produced it. In the latter case, the technique of awareness and observation, even as supported by the additional component of
understanding, does not solve the problem. Here, clearly, is a
behavior our sojourner is not going to approve of.

And this is as it should be. We cannot expect that we will
like everything about another culture any more than we approve
of everything about our own. Nor should we force ourselves to
try. Adjustment must not—indeed, it cannot—be purchased at
the expense of our own self-respect. While we must try, at
times, to transcend our conditioning, we must beware of trying
to alter our personalities. If we are not at ease with ourselves,
can we ever be truly at ease with another culture? If we genuinely respect another culture, we must allow ourselves to be ap-
palled by it. "When you come across an alien culture," Hilary

Mantel has written, "you must not automatically respect it. You must sometimes pay it the compliment of hating it."[3]

"To live in India," the novelist Ruth Prawer Jhabvala has observed,

> and be at peace, one must to a very considerable extent become Indian and adopt Indian attitudes, habits, beliefs, assume, if possible, an Indian personality. But how is this possible? And even if it were possible—without cheating oneself—would it be desirable? Should one try to become something other than what one is?[4]

T. E. Lawrence (of Arabia), for one, didn't think so:

> In my case the efforts for three years to live in the dress of Arabs, and to imitate their mental foundation, quitted me of my English self and let me look at the West and its conventions with new eyes; they destroyed it all for me. At the same time I could not sincerely take on the Arab skin; it was an affectation only. Easily was a man made an infidel, but hardly might he be converted to another faith. . . . Sometimes these selves would converse in the void; and then madness was very near, as I believe it would be near the man who could see things through the veils at once of two customs, two educations, two environments.[5]

Certain kinds of Type I incidents, then, will not respond to the technique of awareness alone; in these cases, awareness must be combined with understanding or knowledge. And certain other kinds will resist even this approach. While the numbers of this latter kind of incident are few, we must accept that they exist and be prepared for them (though we should be careful not to relegate behaviors into this category too hastily). In the vast majority of instances, the technique of awareness will serve us well and prevent that inclination toward withdrawal that leads to unsuccessful adjustment. For the rest, we must accept that part of true adjustment is to understand that there will always be some behaviors we will never get used to.

In the meantime we can be cheered by the fact that in at least one respect the practice of awareness does embrace even those behaviors we cannot accept. As we practice awareness and thereby begin to appreciate how strongly conditioning controls our behavior, we accept, if only subconsciously, that the same dynamic is at work in the local people. We may not think very much of the ideology or values which make up the substance of their conditioning—and we may think even less of some of the behaviors they produce—but we cannot deny the legitimacy of the process: the natives, like us, come by their offensive habits honestly. And this realization allows us to separate individuals from their actions, to deplore the deeds and still have compassion for the doers.

Now let us consider the problem of adjustment from the perspective of Type II incidents, wherein it is our behavior that causes the offense and the local people who are trying to avoid us. The problem with Type II incidents is to become aware of them. If we knew we were committing a cultural gaffe, we would stop. And yet not knowing, how *can* we stop? With Type I incidents we have our feelings—of frustration, anger, etc.—to alert us to our behavior (once we've trained ourselves, that is), but with this second category of incident, we are hard put to discover that our behavior may be alienating the people around us.

It is not realistic, for example, to expect the local people to tell us when we've made a gaffe. Most of us are reluctant to tell people from our own culture that they have caused offense, however well we may know them; how much less likely are we to tell a foreigner? Even if a native should attempt to give us some feedback on our behavior, the effort often goes unrewarded. This is because the act of expressing disfavor is itself culturally conditioned, and the feedback can easily go over our heads or be taken to mean something else. In much of Asia, for example, one does not directly confront another person but communicates a complaint through a third party. The average Westerner is apt to be confused by this indirectness and may not even realize he or she has been rebuked (or may be offended or annoyed that the wronged party didn't have the courage to bring the matter up directly.)

Hugh Brody writes about the difficulty of giving feedback across cultures in his book *The People's Land*, a study of the Eskimos:

> Yet the criticism of individual Whites is rarely ad-
> dressed to the Whites themselves. Eskimos feel a
> deep reluctance to confront Whites, even when in-
> dignation is keen and widespread. Moreover—many
> Eskimos say—Whites do not notice the subtle, quiet
> expressions of criticism they prefer to use.[6]

If you are with a group of Japanese, say, or Thais, and they offer an offhand criticism of Americans in general, chances are they have just given you a piece of personal feedback on something you've done. If they should go on to specifically exempt you from the criticism—"But you aren't like most Americans"— then you can be sure the criticism is aimed at you.

Most sojourners take a direct approach to the problem of Type II incidents: we ask the local people and/or other expatri- ates how a foreigner is supposed to behave. We ask, in other words, to be taught the do's and don't's of the culture. This is by far the most common approach to adjustment and the focus of much cross-cultural training, despite the fact that it ignores al- together the phenomenon of Type I incidents. It is a popular methodology because it appears to meet the sojourner's deepest, most immediate need: to be as comfortable as possible as quickly as possible in the new culture. What quicker or better way than to be told what to do and what not to do in fifteen to twenty of the most common social/business situations? In truth, there is no harm in this strategy, as far as it goes. But it doesn't go very far.

The "do's and don't's" approach is necessarily situational, with all the built-in drawbacks of that genre of problem solving. Only a fixed number of situations can be presented and then only in the most general manner. Contingencies and con- text are ignored. "Don't start talking business with a Saudi," we may be told, "until you've first made considerable small talk about the weather or his health and otherwise spent ten to fif- teen minutes exchanging pleasantries." But what if this is the second or third meeting we have had with that person that day?

What if he's an old friend and obviously in a hurry? What if he's Western-educated or his son has just died or he comes very late to our meeting? As long as we confine ourselves to the situations on our list and so long as those situations unfold according to the script—in short, so long as we only meet the average Saudi (who behaves as he's supposed to)—then this method can be helpful.

By far the most telling limitation of this strategy is its dangerous oversimplification of an extremely complex phenomenon. It is like treating the symptoms but not the disease; we may feel better knowing the do's and don't's, but we are still unprepared. It may boost our confidence, but confidence of just this sort, as any oldtimer can verify, goeth before many a spectacular fall. A cardinal rule of living abroad is to always err on the side of caution.

"It is appropriate," Edward Stewart has written in his book *American Cultural Patterns,*

> to raise the possibility of providing the American going abroad or the foreigner in the United States with a list of do's and don't's. Why not tell the American never to point his feet at a person in Thailand; don't pat a child on the head in Laos; always use polite and flowery expressions in speaking; and do not expect punctuality. In short it should be possible to draw up a list of behaviors ranging from those that are desirable to those that are taboo. This approach, however, is not commendable, for several reasons.
>
> The classification of behavior as desirable or taboo endows it with misleading objectivity. Behavior is ambiguous: the same action may have different meanings in different situations, so that it is necessary to identify the context of behavior and the contingencies of action before the [sojourner] can be armed with prescriptions for specific acts. Fulfillment of this strategy is impossible since the [number] of possible events is [unlimited].
>
> Effective behavior [abroad] can only emerge from sound cross-cultural understanding.[7]

We should also be wary of asking the natives how we are supposed to act; they may have a lot to say, but we need not pay too much attention. What comes out of the horse's mouth is widely overrated. The people who live a culture make notoriously poor guides to it; they don't have the necessary objectivity. And if we do question the natives, or, just as likely, they volunteer their explanations, we must be careful not to generalize from the advice of one or two. What they say may be true for people of their own age group, level of education, and socioeconomic background (not to mention caste, religion, region or locality, sex, and experience) but not for other sectors of society. Ask a Montana rancher and a Manhattan banker what proper behavior or dress is at a dinner party and try to generalize from their answers!

What are we to do? We can't sense when we have done wrong, the local people won't tell us (or, if they do, we may not realize we have been told), and it's difficult to discover what is right. In fact there is nothing more we can do to solve the puzzle of Type II incidents other than to keep applying the technique of awareness we have already described. It is through this method, after all, that we learn what to expect of the natives in various situations. *And the way the local people behave in any given situation is, of course, how we should behave.* Thus it is that as we learn what to expect from Tunisians, we are, perforce, learning what Tunisians expect from us. In creating the circumstances for observing objectively how the local people behave at the post office or at a meal or during a business meeting, we are teaching ourselves—albeit subconsciously—how to behave in those exact same situations.

The technique of awareness also prepares us for dealing with Type II incidents in two other respects: it conditions us to be wary of our instincts and it instills in us the habit of observing. These two factors are significant, for merely paying attention during Type I encounters can't prepare us for all the situations wherein we might make Type II mistakes; many Type II situations have no Type I counterpart that could serve, as it were, as a training opportunity. We would not, for example, consider our meal with a Moroccan family a Type I incident; that is, we would not experience it as frustrating or stressful (though they might) and therefore be inclined to gain control over our reaction, observe the situation, and thus learn what was expected of us the next time around. On the other hand, if we work at developing the skills of objective observation and what we might call "instinct override"—the ability to look and then look again before acting—we would approach an evening such as this with more caution and circumspection and perhaps sidestep some of the more obvious culture traps. This all has to be in moderation, however; if we carry this circumspection too far and sacrifice naturalness and spontaneity on the altar of cultural correctness, we aren't likely to have a very good time or, for that matter, to ever be invited back.

Virtually everyone in the field of intercultural communication agrees on one essential point: the necessity of objectively observing the culture around us and learning therefrom. This is sound advice—which we have reiterated here—but it is fundamentally incomplete. Moreover, it misses the point. It glosses over the fact that human beings are not naturally given to (some would say we aren't even capable of) objective observation. When we observe, we instinctively respond to the content of what we see: it pleases us; it appalls us; it excites, frightens, angers, shocks, embarrasses, or saddens us. And this response, from the moment it arises, colors all subsequent observation. Unless this subjective element can somehow be purged from our behavior, truly objective observation—and all that it has to teach us—must remain forever beyond our reach.

That is why we have insisted in these pages on the concept of awareness, for it is only by becoming aware of our emotional states (the subjective element) that we are able to cut off our responses to the culture outside ourselves and thereby create an interlude wherein we can truly see what we are observing. If we are to learn from what we see, we must, paradoxically, remove ourselves from the process.

REFERENCES

1. Philip Glazebrook, *Journey to Kars*, 181–82.

2. Fatima Mernissi, *Beyond the Veil: Male-Female Dynamics in a Modern Muslim Society* (Cambridge, MA.: Schenken Publishing Co., 1975), 81–86.

3. Hilary Mantel, "Last Morning in Al Hamra," *Spectator*, 24 January 1987, 26.

4. Ruth Prawer Jhabvala, *Out of India* (New York: Simon and Schuster, 1987), 21.

5. T. E. Lawrence, *The Seven Pillars of Wisdom* (London: The Reprint Society, 1939), 30.

6. Hugh Brody, *The People's Land* 156.

7. Edward Stewart, *American Cultural Patterns: A Cross-Cultural Perspective* (Yarmouth, ME: Intercultural Press, 1972), 20–21.

■ 6 ■

A WILD SURREALIST CONFUSION

Two nervous clergymen travelling on a Danube
steamer reported to the papers dreadful atrocities
on every hand, a perfect forest of Bulgar
Christians impaled on stakes as far as the eye
could see, and much fury against the Turk was
expended until it was pointed out that these
"Christians" were more probably bundles of fodder
spiked up out of reach of the stock, as had been
the Balkan way of doing the thing for any
number of centuries.

—PHILIP GLAZEBROOK
Journey to Kars

In chapter 5 we presented an outline of the technique of awareness. In this chapter we will examine certain features of this
technique more closely and consider some of the implications of
practicing it.

It would be misleading to claim that without practicing
awareness people would be unable to adapt to unfamiliar situations. At least in the sense we have used the word here, most of
us are unaware most of the time, yet we regularly encounter situations in our daily lives that our past experience hasn't prepared us for but with which we nevertheless manage to cope.
We encounter these situations, we react and tend to withdraw,
and then, over time, as we encounter them again and again, we
take in more of what is happening, we react less, and we grow

used to them. In a word, we adapt. Why should we do anything different when we go abroad?

What is different about being overseas, the reason we cannot continue to rely on the natural adjustment process, is not that this process suddenly stops or that we encounter any fundamentally different kind of new situation, but that we encounter new situations *on a scale* we have never known before. The nearly continuous barrage of new experiences served up by the unfamiliar country and culture (to say nothing of the new job and the new community) during our early months overseas triggers a correspondingly intense wave of reaction and anxiety and an unusually strong urge to withdraw. The scale of the stimulus, the intensity of our reaction, the degree to which we are prompted to withdraw, and the length of time it takes before we begin to feel comfortable enough to venture back into the culture—these considerations combined with the fact that we will probably not live in a given country more than two or three years, are what make it necessary for us to intervene in the process of adjustment and hurry it along. Awareness, or what we might call the conscious manipulation of our built-in adjustment apparatus, may not be essential to cultural adaptation, but it is essential to speeding it up. And if we don't adapt quickly overseas, for the reasons we have given above, we may never adapt at all.

This difference in scale might be compared to the difference between how we would feel meeting one person we didn't know and meeting an entire room of people we didn't know. In the first instance we would experience a certain uneasiness and hesitancy and be reluctant to do or say very much, not knowing how the stranger might react. We would withdraw somewhat into ourselves and try to get a sense of the other person. Eventually, after more contact with the individual (at that or subsequent meetings), we would learn what he or she is like and feel more at ease. In the second instance, we would be noticeably more uneasy and hesitant, much more reluctant to speak and act, inclined to withdraw even further into ourselves, and all but certain to take much longer to get to know the various individuals and feel comfortable among them.

Left to our own devices, we would take some time to get to know the roomful of strangers. But what if circumstances dictated that we must get to know this group of people quickly, before the end of the evening? Then we would have to take matters into our own hands and make a conscious effort to overcome our uneasiness at approaching so many strangers, and systematically go about befriending them. This is essentially the case when we go abroad and why, therefore, we can't trust our instincts to be up to the job. (Incidentally, the room down the hall that is full of people we know is, of course, the expatriate colony.)

The technique of awareness relies heavily on our being able to observe objectively what is happening around us, to receive impressions from our surroundings, which then form the basis for what we expect the next time we are in a like situation. This is straightforward enough, but it is not as easy as it sounds: just as, by the laws of conditioning, we can't expect people to behave in ways we have never experienced, neither can we observe behavior we've never seen before. There are any number of behaviors the local people exhibit that we are not capable of seeing, or, more accurately, that technically we may *see*, but that we do not recognize as having any significance or meaning. Needless to say, this can make observing what is happening around us—and learning therefrom—a tricky business.

Would we, if we weren't told, realize that in the South Pacific a belch following a drink from a coconut was a polite necessity rather than a random escape of gas? Would we understand, watching our Hindu friend arrange his bedroll, that he was trying to position himself so as not to be pointing his feet at anyone's head (instead of trying to get near the window or away from the door)?

And how much of the following would we see at a tea shop along the trail in Nepal? Would we notice that our porter (from a low caste) doesn't actually enter under the roof of the shop but sits just outside; that the lady making the tea lets us take our cup from her hand but sets the porter's on the ground, whence he collects it; that she cleans our cup herself but pours water into his, lets him rinse it out once and set it on the ground, then pours more water in and rinses it out a second time herself? Would we notice, handing our porter a box of matches, that he doesn't take them from us, but cups his hands to receive them? Most of these actions, if they struck us at all, would seem perfectly arbitrary. As a rule, we only see that which has meaning for us, and the only behavior that has meaning for us is that with which we are already familiar, that we have seen before. "It is a repeated finding," Edward Stewart notes, "that perceptual responses are influenced by the individual's expectations. To an extent not usually recognized, perception resides in the perceiver not in the external world."[1]

C. S.Lewis makes much the same point in *Out of the Silent Planet* (appendix 2):

> He gazed about him and the very intensity of his desire to take in the new world at a glance defeated itself. He saw nothing but colours—colours that refused to form themselves into things. Moreover, he knew nothing yet well enough to see it; you cannot see things until you know roughly what they are.[2]

"It is one of my regrets," Edmund Taylor writes in a similar vein in his book, *Richer by Asia*,

> that I have not yet learned to see an Indian village or a bazaar; my eyes aren't trained, and I couldn't describe one to save my life. I love them and am endlessly fascinated; but all I can make out is a wild surrealist confusion of men and animals and many kinds of inanimate objects, arranged in completely implausible patterns.[3]

There's a nearly exact equivalent in the case of learning a foreign language. When we listen to someone speaking a foreign tongue we can only hear those words we already know and the rest is mere noise. Similarly, in observing the behavior of foreigners, we can only pick out those actions we already know—that mean something in our culture (though they may not mean the same thing or anything at all in the local culture)—and all the rest, rich in meaning to everyone but us, is just random, undifferentiated movement.

How, then, can we learn from our observations if we can't make any sense out of what we are seeing? What actually happens when we observe a phenomenon for the first time is that we immediately see any familiar elements there may be in the scene—in this instance, any behavior that is not peculiar to the culture—and they form a context, bracketing the unfamiliar elements, the meaning of which we then try to guess from this context. It is much the same process that occurs when we are reading and come across a word we don't know; we guess at the meaning from the context. In addition, the actions we observe, whether we understand them or not, still make an impression, however dim, on our consciousness, so that we recognize them on subsequent viewings; and a pattern, albeit incomprehensible, begins to emerge. We know we've seen those actions before, even if we don't yet know what they mean.

All this happens naturally; there's nothing to do except to try to observe the scene with as much objectivity as possible. If we have first cut off our reaction to the scene, then we will not be distracted by our emotional state and will be able to give our full attention to observing.

The sojourner should be aware of two other obstacles to seeing. Not only is there behavior we cannot see, there is also behavior we see quite readily but which doesn't mean the same thing in both cultures, behavior, in short, that we misinterpret. In India, shaking one's head from side to side means yes. In Morocco and other Moslem countries it is the custom for men to walk hand in hand in the street. In Tonga the shopkeeper who raises her eyebrows at you isn't flirting; she is just answering yes to your question about whether her shop sells sugar. "Moreover," J. G Farrell writes in *The Hill Station,*

> I wish my eyes were better able to see the differences. . . . I see things without understanding them. It took me ages to realize that what appeared to be splashes of blood all over the pavement of Bombay was merely people spitting betel juice.[4]

The Indian writer Vikram Seth in *From Heaven Lake* had a similar experience on a visit to China:

> We examine the wares of the pavement hawkers; dates and figs and grapes and vegetables as well as an assortment of clothes and shoes, utensils and other household goods. I buy something that looks like a crude wooden pipe from a Uighur woman, who holds up three fingers to indicate the price. It will make a good present for a smoker friend, I think, and on impulse buy two more, asking, in a

> mixture of Chinese and puffing gestures, whether I
> am holding it properly. The woman looks at me
> with incomprehension. A small crowd gathers, as it
> usually does around something as entertaining as a
> foreigner making a purchase, but there is an under-
> current of hilarity that I cannot fathom. Only later
> do I learn that the "pipe" is a device for diverting a
> baby's urine out of its cot so that it does not soil the
> bedclothes.[5]

In these instances when we misinterpret behavior or phe-
nomena, we can often discover our mistake by checking
the context to see if it is consistent with our conclusions. When
the Indian shakes his head from side to side, does anything
else about his manner—the look on his face, his body language—suggest agreement or disagreement? Do the Moroccan
men otherwise seem attracted to each other in a romantic
way? Are most other men behaving similarly? Does any other
behavior by the Tongan girl support her sudden, unexpected
flirtatiousness?

Then there's the problem of seeing what isn't there—when a
certain piece of behavior means something in our culture but
has no meaning in the local one. The raised middle finger, an
obscene gesture in America, has no significance in most other
cultures. Once again, we can usually tell from the context—
does the fellow seem particularly agitated otherwise?—whether
our interpretation is correct.

There is a similar problem of hearing. Just as we may not see
much of what happens around us, neither do we always hear or
interpret correctly much of what is said to us (in our own language). Westerners, who generally speak their mind, don't realize that when a Thai, cautiously and with considerable
hesitation, suggests a certain course of action, he is in fact expressing the strongest possible wish that that course be adopted
and will be upset if it isn't. If he were neutral about a proposal
or only moderately in favor, he wouldn't bring it up at all (and
would expect you to know what his silence meant). In the same
way, when a Japanese friend says she is going to fix a meal and
asks if you'd like to join her, she has just politely invited you to
leave. The notorious indirectness of Asians may, to a large ex-

tent, be nothing more than our inability to recognize Asian-style directness when we see it.

There is, quite literally, more to a foreign culture than meets the eye. And sometimes less. While we can't always trust what we see, this need not diminish the luster of observation as the preeminent tool for learning about another culture; we simply have to be aware that at least some of what we see may only be in the eye of the beholder.

Just as there is adjustment, so also there is overadjustment, the spectacle of going native. Like its opposite number, withdrawing into the expatriate colony, going native is an inappropriate response to living abroad. Nor should it be confused with genuine adjustment.

Going native is the syndrome wherein the expatriate throws over his own culture in a fit of enthusiasm for the local one, embracing its strictures with an eagerness that is often perplexing to the true natives. The sojourner mimics the ways of the natives (often to an exaggerated extent), is uncritically accepting of everything about native society, and pointedly has nothing to do with anything or anyone from his or her birth culture.

It's a pose. Apart from that curious (and largely bygone) breed of oldtimers who came out to Tonga or the Congo or Brazil some twenty or thirty years ago and somehow never left, most of those who go native are shamming. What drives them is not so much a genuine attraction to the native culture, but a confused antipathy toward their own. They aren't making a choice as much as they are making a statement. This is evident in the speed with which the average candidate goes over to the other side, usually after only two or three months in the new country, making it unlikely that the individual knows the local culture well enough to legitimately prefer it.

Going native is as inappropriate and unhealthy a response to the overseas experience as disappearing into the expatriate sub-culture. It is as illogical to prefer everything about the native culture as it is to prefer everything about one's own. And both reactions are nurtured by the same factors: an ignorance of the local culture and an ever deeper indulgence in self-deception. Nor is going native understood or welcomed by the real natives;

they can accept that foreigners might cling to their own ways and reject those of the natives, but they can't help being suspicious of people who so effortlessly doff their own identity to embrace one they can't possibly appreciate.

Not everything about cultural adjustment is harder or more complex than it first appears. In at least one respect it's actually easier than we might think—easier because we've done it before, whether we've ever left our native shores or not. "Culture shock is everywhere," Pierre Casse has written,

> There is no need to move to an esoteric, strange culture to experience it. It occurs each time that a contradiction or confrontation between various values, beliefs, and assumptions is experienced. It can be superficial and unnoticed. Sometimes it is drastic and leads to some kind of psychological trauma. It can be caused by the change of the value system of an organization as well as by the discovery of one's own real self.[6]

If you live in rural Vermont and spend the summer with your grandparents in Boston or New York City, you leave one culture and enter quite another, experiencing that same shock and anxiety the expatriate feels in a foreign country. "It was like entering another, more nationalistic country," Jan Morris writes,

> like entering France, say, out of Switzerland. The moment I crossed the Red River out of Oklahoma the nationality of Texas assaulted me, almost xenophobically, and I seemed to be passing into another sensibility, another historical experience, another set of values, perhaps.[7]

You adapt to a new culture when you leave home and go away to college (and when you come back at Christmas). There's one culture at the office and another at home. You change cultures when you marry or become a parent, when you get a new boss, when a spouse or parent or child dies. These are all experiences of transition and its associated stresses, when you are obliged to give up or moderate certain habits and get used to new ones. Thus it is that we already have many of the skills we need to function overseas. Indeed, if we didn't, the shock of going to another country would be unendurable. All we need is to begin applying these skills—with a vengeance—in our new setting.

It is, of course, not merely the expatriate who encounters and must learn to live with foreigners; those who stay at home are liable to encounter sojourners from abroad. Moreover, we are increasingly likely to encounter them in circumstances where it is prudent, even necessary, that we understand and get along with them. While we need not concern ourselves so much with German or Japanese tour groups (unless we work in the hotel or restaurant business), if we work for Nissan in Tennessee or teach college in Michigan (or Maine or Montana), we may have a Japanese boss, an Indian colleague, or a class of Korean, Taiwanese, and Kuwaiti undergraduates. Whether as colleagues, clients, or superiors, foreigners play an ever increasing part in our daily lives and often exercise direct control over our livelihood. Given these conditions, we are all but certain to encounter and perpetrate the kinds of cultural incidents we've described in these pages. And it behooves us, accordingly, to educate ourselves in this matter of cultural sensitivity. Boorishness is no longer the luxury of the stay-at-home.

Adjusting at home, to the foreigners in our midst, is essentially the same as adjusting abroad, to the natives all around us; the difference is one of degree rather than of kind. There are several mitigating factors. For one thing, the sheer number of incidents, of either type, is much lower in the home culture. For another, the stakes of not adjusting aren't nearly so high; that is, we don't run the risk of adopting the unwholesome lifestyle of the foreign colony or of having to pick up and relocate halfway around the world. Yet another difference is the absence of any competing demands, such as getting used to a new community, a new job, and a new country.

We should also remember that even as we struggle to understand the sojourners among us, they are likewise struggling to meet us halfway, educating themselves, as best they can, in American mores and adjusting their behavior accordingly. And we might add that to the extent we understand the phenomenon of crossing cultures described herein, to that degree we can forgive the sojourners their mistakes and temper our judgments.

Otherwise, the essential cross-cultural dynamic remains unchanged: foreigners in our country behave in ways which put us off and we do the same to them. To rectify the situation, we must train ourselves to be aware of our reactions, to appreciate their provenance, and in the ensuing interlude of objectivity to observe closely what is happening. Properly reconditioned, we will come to expect of foreigners none other than that behavior which—*mirabile dictu*—they naturally exhibit.

REFERENCES

1. Edward Stewart, *American Cultural Patterns*, 15.

2. C. S. Lewis, *Out of the Silent Planet* (New York: Macmillan, 1965), 41–42.

3. Edmond Taylor, *Richer By Asia* (New York: Time/Life, 1964), 67.

4. J. G. Farrell, *The Hill Station* (London: Futura, 1987), 211.

5. Vikram Seth, *From Heaven Lake* (London: Chatto and Windus, 1984), 12.

6. Pierre Casse, *Training for the Cross-Cultural Mind*, xiii.

7. Jan Morris, "Trans-Texas," *Journeys* (Oxford: Oxford University Press, 1984), 111.

■ 7 ■

THE TOWER OF
BABEL

We travelled in a big truck through the nation of
France on our way to Belgium, and every time
we passed through a little town, we'd see these
signs "Boulangerie," "Patisserie," and "Rue" this
and "Rue" that, and rue the day you came here
young man. When we got to our hundred and
eightieth French village, I screamed at the top of
my lungs, "The joke is over! English, please!" I
couldn't believe a whole country couldn't speak
English. One-third of a nation, all right, but not
a whole country.

—MEL BROOKS
in Show People by Kenneth Tynan

It's a funny thing; the French call it a *couteau*,
the Germans call it a *messer*, but we call it a
knife, which is after all what it really is.

—RICHARD JENKYNS
The Victorians and Ancient Greece

Sometime in 1906 I was walking in the heat of
the day through the Bazaars. As I passed an Arab
Cafe, in no hostility to my straw hat but desiring
to shine before his friends, a fellow called out in
Arabic, "God curse your father, O Englishman." I
was young then and quicker tempered, and could

85

not refrain from answering in his own language that
I would also curse his father if he were in a position
to inform me which of his mother's two and ninety
admirers his father had been. I heard footsteps behind
me, and slightly picked up the pace, angry with
myself for committing the sin Lord Cromer would not
pardon—a row with Egyptians. In a few seconds I felt
a hand on each arm. "My brother," said the original
humorist, "return and drink with us coffee and smoke
(in Arabic one speaks of 'drinking' smoke). I did not
think that your worship knew Arabic, still less the
correct Arabic abuse, and we would fain benefit
further by your important thoughts."

—RONALD STORRS
Orientations

When the tower of Babel fell
It caused a lot of unnecessary Hell.
Personal rapport
Became a complicated bore
And a lot more difficult than it had been before,
When the tower of Babel fell.

—NOEL COWARD
Collected Lyrics

Rare are the expatriates who speak the language of the country
they live in. As learning the local tongue is normally not essential to functioning on the job or in the community and as
achieving minimal fluency in another language requires considerable time and effort, most sojourners forego the experience.
Even those earnest, well-intended sorts who immediately go out
and find a tutor usually fall by the wayside two or three months
down the road. They are still keen on learning Swahili, you
understand, but they're just too busy. "One of these days he
must simply get down to the language," muses one of Anthony
Burgess' characters. "There never seemed to be time,
somehow."[1]
    While knowing the language may not be critical to living in
another country, no one would dispute that even a minimal

grasp of the local tongue significantly increases the expatriate's effectiveness. Similarly, while speaking the language may not be essential to successful cultural adjustment, it certainly expedites the process. In this chapter we will briefly review some of the advantages of learning the local language (for those whose circumstances don't require it). It may be true that many expatriates don't have time for language lessons, but it's also possible that all those tasks they are so busy with would go more smoothly—and take less time—if they did.

One of the more immediate and deeply felt advantages of learning the local language is the sense of well-being and security it provides. Those who cannot speak the language of the country wherein they reside and whose inhabitants can't speak theirs can never feel altogether at ease. There is the ever present possibility that they may suddenly find themselves in situations where they cannot make themselves understood, where, for want of being able to express their needs, those needs must go unmet. Who hasn't had the experience of going to a shop and leaving without the desired item for lack of being able to describe it (or spot it on the shelf)? And how much more serious is the issue if it is medicine one is after, or one is lost or there has been an accident and help is urgently needed. The spectre of these scenarios can be deeply troubling to the average expatriate, giving rise to feelings of profound vulnerability. "When I was thus suddenly cast on foreign land," Edward Gibbon recalls in his *Memoirs*,

> I found myself deprived of the use of speech and
> hearing; and, during some weeks, incapable not only
> of enjoying the pleasures of conversation, but even
> of asking or answering a question in the common
> intercourse of life. . . . From a man I was again de
> graded to the dependence of a schoolboy . . . and
> helpless and awkward as I have ever been. My con
> dition seemed as destitute of hope as it was devoid of
> pleasure. [2]

Related to this sense of helplessness is the loss of self-esteem that comes with the inability to converse in the local language. Average, articulate adults—capable in so many other ways— who are suddenly transformed into virtual mutes, who can only nod and smile foolishly when addressed by well-intentioned, monolingual locals, find the experience demeaning. For all their competence, they feel—and in a sense, are—inferior to the three-year-old neighbor child who may still wet his pants but at least knows how to count to ten. It's an open question who might fare better in a tight spot.

In *Living Poor,* his classic book about the Peace Corps, Moritz Thomsen captures the feeling exactly:

> On this trip to Machala to catch the coastal steamer for Guayaquil, I made my first close emotional contact with a national. . . . He got on the bus somewhere up in the mountains above La Toma, or rather he was poured onto the bus by some friends of his who, I'm convinced, were glad to see him go—a man of about forty with a foxy little black moustache and quick, black buttonhole eyes. There was no place for him to sit on the bus, so he squatted in the aisle, put his head in my lap, and quietly passed out. The bus rushed down the mountain, vibrating and pulsating, and my friend gradually sifted onto the floor, where he slept for a couple of hours. He awoke suddenly, after one particularly spectacular bump had thrown him about three feet in the air, and found himself staring into the face of a gringo.

> He was thunderstruck. His face took on an expression of loving kindness; it was obvious he loved gringos. He began to pat my head. And he began to talk. He talked a torrent of Spanish at me, but I could scarcely understand perfect Castilian enunciated clearly and slowly by some Spanish Richard Burton, let alone the coastal patois with its slurred and jazzy sounds, all well mixed with sleep and alcohol. My God, I couldn't understand a word he said, not one single word, and I had to sit there mile after mile, smiling like a dummy, surreptitiously wiping off the flecks of spit that he enthusiastically directed at my face. The other passengers were watching me with expressions of increasing pity as it dawned on them, one by one, that the gringo was a half-wit. My friend finally realized it too and gazed at me with a baffled look on his face. It was a look of anguish for me—for me, the escaped but harmless crackbrain, wandering lost, dazed, and speechless in a

> strange and distant country. To tell you the truth, for about three hours on that wild plunge to the coastal tropics, this was exactly how I saw myself.[3]

Reeling from incidents such as these, most expatriates, like the rest of us, try to run away. They withdraw into the safe, comforting world of the foreign colony where one can always make oneself understood and where one stands at least an even chance of being master of the situation. The dynamic, as we have seen, is self-sustaining; not speaking the language, sojourners feel insecure and withdraw into the expatriate world where, needless to say, their command of the language does not improve.

Another reason for learning the language is that in the process, as a kind of by-product or bonus, we learn about the culture as well, for culture is not only manifest in how people behave, but also in how they express themselves. The sojourner who takes up the study of Arabic enters the world of Islam just as surely as the tourist passing through the gates of the Kasbah. "Fortunately," observes a character in Gore Vidal's *Creation,*

> Caraka knew enough Aryan words to help me begin to comprehend not only a new language but a new world, for it is the language of a people that tells us most about what gods they worship and what sort of men they are or would like to be.[4]

The student of Arabic, for example, learns that "God willing" (N'sha'llah) is automatically added to any statement about the future (just as "thanks be to God" accompanies any reference to fortunate events of the past), that many common given names—Abdullah, Abdeslam, Abdelwahid—translate as slave (*abd*) of God, appreciating, as a consequence, the essential fatalism of Arab culture. Similarly, the student of Nepali, struggling to sort out the myriad nouns for family members—there are four words for uncle, denoting whether the man in question is the brother of one's father or mother and whether he is older or younger than said parent—readily appreciates the importance of the family in Nepali society and may even intuit the relative insignificance of the individual. (In this regard, what does the common American usage of "old man," for father, tell a foreigner about us?)

Paul Scott finds even subtler evidence of culture in language. "Hindi," he writes,

> is spare and beautiful. In it we can think thoughts that have the merit of simplicity and truth and convey these thoughts in correspondingly spare, simple, truthful images. English is not spare. It cannot be called truthful because its subtleties are infinite. It is the language of a people who have probably earned their reputation for perfidy and hypocrisy because their language itself is so flexible, so light-headed.[5]

But the most compelling reason to learn the language of another land is because of the symbolic significance of the act of communication. At its most fundamental, the attempt to speak with people in a foreign country is an acknowledgement of their humanity and individual worth (as it is, perforce, an indication of our own), a sign that we take them and their concerns seriously. And the gesture is as important as our degree of proficiency . What matters is not what we say when we speak Arabic or Nepali, or how well we say it, but what making the effort to speak Arabic or Nepali says about us.

"Learning a native language," Charles Allen writes, "was perhaps the best thing that ever happened to people who went out to India, and those who failed to do so remained forever at a distance from the land and its people."[6]

REFERENCES

1. Anthony Burgess, *The Long Day Wanes: A Malayan Trilogy*, 24.

2. Edward Gibbon, *Memoirs*, excerpted in Hugh and Pauline Massingham, comps., *The Englishman Abroad* (Gloucester, UK: Alan Sutton, 1984), 15.

3. Moritz Thomsen, *Living Poor* (Seattle: University of Washington Press, 1969), 23–24.

4. Gore Vidal, *Creation* (New York: Random House, 1981), 134.

5. Paul Scott, *The Jewel in the Crown*, 215.

6. Charles Allen, *Plain Tales from the Raj*, 75.

8

THE END OF ALL OUR EXPLORING

Father, Mother, and Me,
  Sister and Auntie say
All the people like us are We,
  And everyone else is They.
And They live over the sea
  While we live over the way,
But—would you believe it?—They look upon We
  As only a sort of They!

We eat pork and beef
  With cow-horn-handled knives.
They who gobble Their rice off a leaf
  Are horrified out of Their lives;
While They who live up a tree,
  Feast on grubs and clay,
(Isn't it scandalous?) look upon We
  As a simply disgusting They!

We eat kitcheny food.
  We have doors that latch.
They drink milk and blood
  Under an open thatch. We have doctors to fee.
  They have wizards to pay.
And (impudent heathen!) They look upon We
  As a quite impossible They!

All good people agree,
  And all good people say,

> All nice people, like us, are We
> And everyone else is They:
> But if you cross over the sea,
> Instead of over the way,
> You may end by (think of it!) looking on We
> As only a sort of They!
>
> —RUDYARD KIPLING
> "We and They"

Adjusting to another culture requires a major, sustained effort under less than ideal circumstances; people don't shed their instincts and change their behavior without a struggle. But the effort will be handsomely rewarded. Just *how* is the subject of this chapter.

Perhaps the most obvious consequence of successful adjustment is that we foreigners become increasingly effective in our work. It is axiomatic—and inevitable—that the better we understand the behavior of the local people the more easily we can work with them. The success of any interaction, in or outside our own culture, rests primarily on our ability to anticipate the behavior of others, including their reactions to our behavior. If we cannot do this, as we often cannot overseas, then even the possibility of successful interaction is largely precluded.

A related matter here is that the better the sojourner understands the local culture, the harder it is for the natives to hide behind it. The Filipino district agricultural agent who doesn't want the bother of managing a pilot erosion project can always find a cultural explanation for why the local farmers won't go along with such an innovation. And who is the average foreigner, even if there is suspicion of a trick, to call the agent's bluff? The sojourner who has adapted, however, who knows the culture and therefore knows better, will see the agent's game and make short work of it. Indeed, if the agent is perceptive or knows the sojourner, he won't waste his time trying to fool him.

In this context it is interesting to note that the Japanese, unlike many peoples, do not always appreciate it when a foreigner speaks their language well. Part of the reason is that fluency in the language allows the foreigner to penetrate the public persona the Japanese so carefully cultivate and come to know the individual personality beneath. This in turn cancels the natural advantage the notoriously formal Japanese have in dealing with outsiders, particularly Westerners, who wear their thoughts and feelings on their sleeves. It is possible that the Japanese record of success in business is as much a function of their infamous inscrutability as their way with lasers and microchips.

Another consequence of cultural adjustment is the sense of security it allows us to feel. Ignorance is the breeding ground of fear and anxiety. Not knowing what the natives will do next or how they will react to what we next do produces a constant tension and feeling of uneasiness. We can never be altogether confident or comfortable, never free of the almost palpable suspicion that what we don't know can indeed hurt us.

On a deeper level the process of coming to know another culture allows us to gradually become ourselves again. Many of us, not knowing which of our behaviors may be culturally acceptable (or neutral) and which may not, err on the side of caution and move through intercultural situations in a state of semiparalysis, earnestly practicing the greatest possible self-restraint; we do and, in particular, we say nothing that may reflect badly on us. We are, quite literally, not ourselves. The strain this effort causes, not to mention the energy it consumes, may be nothing compared to the resentment it can make us feel toward the circumstances—that is, the culture—that oblige us to act in this unnatural fashion. But worst of all is the feeling that comes over us that we are somehow losing touch with who we are. It is likely that at least part of that loneliness and sense of isolation we feel overseas may not be the result of missing relatives and friends, but of feeling estranged from our own inner selves.

Once we begin to understand the culture, however, we learn what is appropriate and what is not and accordingly release our grip on our instincts and let our personalities loose. The relief we feel is enormous, and the local people, not incidentally, find it much easier to be with us.

The natives undergo a similar metamorphosis once we begin to understand their culture: that is, they too become themselves. They have been that all along, of course, but not to us. Until we know the local culture reasonably well, we can never be sure, in our dealings with individuals, which behaviors of theirs are mandated by the culture and which are peculiar to them as individuals. If a colleague is hurt when we fail to remember her birthday, is it because the culture sets great store by birthdays (and we'd better not forget those of our other colleagues either) or is it merely that Rosita is particularly sensitive—a useful piece of information if it is true? When we shout at a merchant who won't take back a defective lamp, are we being boorish by reacting to an accepted cultural practice or is the man in fact a cheat (at whom the locals would also shout) whom we'd be foolish to indulge? Until we know the culture, we can never be sure.

But once we do, our experience abroad is radically transformed. Indeed, in many ways it is only at this point that our experience abroad truly begins. We can now separate the individual from his or her culture or, more accurately, distinguish individuals within the culture. Suddenly, everyone has a personality; we like—or, rather, we are free to like—certain people and not others. And we understand that we must treat Ram in one manner and Kumar in another. We can begin to have personal relationships with people or have more—or sometimes less—confidence in those relationships we may already have established. And as the people we know are revealed more clearly to us, we in turn are comfortable in revealing more of ourselves to them.

An even greater consequence of learning about another culture is that in the process we learn a great deal about our own. At home we are rarely prompted to reflect on our cultural selves; we are too busy manifesting our behavior to examine it, and even if we were thus inclined, what would we use as our vantage point?

Once we encounter another frame of reference, however, we begin to see what we never could before. When we notice the unusual behavior of a foreigner, we are at that moment noticing our own behavior as well. We only notice a difference (something unusual) in reference to a norm or standard (the usual) and that norm we refer to is invariably our own behavior. Thus it is that through daily contact with the customs and habits of people from a foreign culture, our attention is repeatedly focused on our own customs and habits; that in encountering another culture, we simultaneously and for the first time encounter our own. It is only a slight exaggeration to say that the average expatriate, even the average tourist, returns from a stay abroad knowing more about his or her own country than about the one just visited. "We shall not cease from exploration," T. S. Eliot wrote in *Four Quartets*,

> And the end of all our exploring
> Will be to arrive where we started
> And know the place for the first time.[1]

Lawrence Durrell felt the same: "Journeys," he writes, "lead us not only outwards in space, but inwards as well. Travel can be one of the most rewarding forms of introspection."[2]

It would be difficult to exaggerate the significance of this inward journey. Living abroad presents us with a unique opportunity for self-discovery and, thereby, for self-improvement. Each of us has in effect two personalities: an individual one that is the product of the particular circumstances of our lives and which accounts for how we are different from those around us and a cultural one which is the product of cultural conditioning and accounts for how we are the same as everyone around us. And each of these personalities (or aspects of our personalities) is the source of wholesome and unwholesome behavior. When we are made aware of these behaviors, we can try to cultivate the former and eradicate the latter. But while we can come to know and change our individual selves without leaving our own culture (through interacting with other individuals), we cannot come to know our cultural selves without benefit of an equivalent vantage point. Thus it is that until we go abroad or otherwise spend time with foreigners, this cultural self lies beyond our awareness, directing and influencing our behavior in ways we can only guess at. But if we go overseas and take the trouble to encounter the local culture, we come face to face with our cultural personality; we meet the stranger within us and come to know him. "Those who go abroad," Edmond Taylor writes,

> step out of their own culture into an alien one and
> begin to look at their own civilization as foreign,
> only to discover how much it influences personal
> life.[3]

Perhaps the most important consequence of pursuing adjustment is the fate it saves us from. Life in the expatriate subculture can be an unwholesome proposition. The forced conviviality, the routine putting down of the natives (about whom, after all, we know very little), the correspondingly inflated opinions one has of ourselves and our compatriots, the sense of regret over missed opportunities (which is best suppressed), the ever greater retreat from reality—all the measures we must take to sustain morale (and belief) in the foreign colony can do permanent damage to our ability to function as sympathetic, compassionate human beings. When we withdraw from the culture around us, we not only isolate ourselves from the local people, but from our own humanity as well.

In another context, Vincent Crapanzano has chronicled this same phenomenon. If we substitute *withdrawing* for his *waiting*, we have an accurate description of the true cost of maladjustment:

> In the very ordinary act of waiting, particularly of waiting in fear, men and women lose what John Keats called "negative capability," the capability of so negating their identity as to be imaginatively open to the complex and never very certain reality around them. Instead, they close off; they create a kind of psychological apartheid, an apartness that in the case of South Africa is institutionally reinforced. In such circumstances there can be no real recognition of the other—no real appreciation of *his* subjectivity. He becomes at once a menial object to be manipulated and a mythic object to be feared. He cannot be counted in his humanity.[4]

We can only hope that when our sojourn is over and we are once again inclined to open ourslves up to others, we will still know how.

On a more hopeful note, we can be cheered by the fact that adjustment—reaching out and trying to understand others—benefits more than just the individual sojourner. It has a residual effect that lingers—in both cultures—long after the expatriate has gone home. "If India and China were amicable towards each other," Vikram Seth has observed,

> almost half the world would be at peace. Yet friendship rests on understanding; and the two countries, despite their contiguity, have had almost no contact

in the course of history. . . . The fact that they are
both part of the same land mass means next to
nothing . . . . The best that can be hoped for on a
national level is a respectful patience on either side.
But on a personal level, to learn about another great
culture is to enrich one's life, to understand one's
own country better, to feel more at home in the
world, and indirectly to add to that reservoir of individual goodwill that may, generations from now,
temper the cynical use of national power.[5]

REFERENCES

1. T. S. Eliot, "Four Quartets," *The Complete Poems and Plays,
   1909–1950* (New York: Harcourt, Brace and World, 1962), 145.

2. Lawrence Durrell, *Bitter Lemons* (New York: E. P. Dutton,
   1957), 15.

3. Edmond Taylor, *Richer by Asia*, xiii.

4. Vincent Crapanzano, *Waiting: The Whites of South Africa* (New
   York: Vintage Books, 1986), xxii.

5. Vikram Seth, *From Heaven Lake*, 177–78.

■ 9 ■

THE REGULAR LIFE

Coming home after some months abroad is very
neurotic.

—ROSE MACAULAY
The Towers of Trebizond

In time all sojourns run their course and expatriates prepare to
go home. Home: where they are no longer foreigners (and where
no one else is either), where they don't have to think before
they speak or act, and where they needn't ever worry again
about having to adjust. Home: where it's easy.

That's the theory, anyway, but the reality is quite different.
"Home," former sojourners will tell you, can take as much getting used to as "abroad" once did. Some would say it takes even
more. In this chapter we will examine reentry and the phenomenon of readjustment, explain why it can be so taxing and offer
some suggestions for coping.

The sting of reentry is not in the adjustments themselves but
in the fact that they're so unexpected. We aren't so much
shocked at *what* it is we have to do, but that we should *have* to
do anything. When we go abroad we expect there will be things
we will have to get used to, but certainly not when we come
home.

In one sense this is true. This is our own culture; we know
how to act here (if we haven't forgotten) and we know what to
expect (though we may be out of practice). We aren't as likely,
then, to alienate or be alienated by others as we are overseas.

But other adjustments abound, and they are all the harder
because we aren't prepared for them. The problem is this word

home. It suggests a place and a life all set up and waiting for us; all we have to do is move in. But home isn't merely a place we inhabit; it's a lifestyle we construct (wherever we go), a pattern of routines, habits, and behaviors associated with certain people, places, and objects—all confined to a limited area or neighborhood. We can certainly construct a home back in our own culture—just as we did abroad—but there won't be one waiting for us when we arrive. And this is true even if you move back into the same house you lived in before you went overseas.

In other words, no one *goes home*; rather, we return to our native country and, in due course, we *create a new home*. This condition of homelessness is perhaps the central characteristic of the experience of reentry, and the confusion, anxiety, and disappointment it arouses in us are the abiding emotions of this difficult period.

Even as we cope with being between homes, we face a number of other adjustments, most of which are reminiscent of the period when we first arrived overseas. We may have to learn (or find) a new job and get used to new colleagues. We may have to adjust to a new climate and learn our way around a new community. And we may miss the company of overseas friends.

We may also miss certain characteristics of life abroad, such as the latitude in behavior (the permissible eccentricities) we are accorded because we are foreigners and don't know any better. "Travel spoils you for the regular life," Bill Barich has written. "When you're moving from country to country in blithe ignorance, you're usually granted the safe passage of an idiot."[1] Many returnees miss being objects of curiosity, the center of local attention, realizing that for all the bother, this made them feel special and, by extension, important. "I was one of the crowd," V. S. Naipaul writes of his first visit to India, his ancestral home,

> In Trinidad to be an Indian was to be distinctive; in Egypt it was more so. Now in Bombay I entered a shop or a restaurant and awaited a special quality of response. And there was nothing. It was like being denied part of my reality. I was faceless. I might sink without a trace into the Indian crowd. . . . Recog-

nition of my difference was necessary to me. I felt
the need to impose myself, and didn't know how.[2]

Beyond that we miss the stimulation of living abroad. For all
its hardships—and largely because of them—life overseas is a
keenly felt experience; there is about it an emotional and intellectual intensity often absent from "regular life." As we encounter the country and the culture around us, trying to make sense
of it, we encounter ourselves as well and revel in the discovery.
We change and grow. We are exhilarated. And we may crave
that exhilaration when we come home. Indeed, it is not uncom-
mon for returned sojourners to cling to certain features of their
overseas life in an attempt to prolong the intensity of the experience. They may eschew certain conveniences or luxuries they
pride themselves on having learned to live without, such as
television or air conditioning, and they may insist on walking
everywhere. And they sometimes spend their early weeks at
home in a concerted effort to locate another overseas posting.

Some returnees actively resist fitting back in, equating it
with a kind of spiritual death. The novelist James Baldwin, who
lived much of his life in Paris, tells of how his father wrote letter
after letter urging his son to come home and "settle down."
Whenever he read those words, Baldwin recalled, they always
made him think of the sediment at the bottom of a stagnant
pond.

The desire to leave "home" becomes all the more acute when
returnees realize how little their compatriots, even their families
and friends, are interested in hearing about their overseas experiences. "When a traveller returneth home," Sir Francis Bacon
wrote, " . . . let him be rather advised in his answers than for-
ward to tell stories."[3]

"I don't think any of us ever spoke about India for the six
months or so we spent in England [on leave]," Vere Birdwood
remembers in *Plain Tales from the Raj*,

> We might occasionally be asked at a dinner, 'Well,
> now, what's all this about old Gandhi?' or something
> of that sort. But to try and settle down for a long
> dissertation [on India] between the soup and the fish
> was not really possible, so we just used to shrug our
> shoulders and our host or hostess or whoever might

have felt obliged to put this question thankfully
passed on to news of the latest theatre in London.[4]

This lack of interest in what may have been one of the sem-
inal experiences of the sojourner's life can be vexing. It's as if
the changes that have taken place in us, the personal growth we
have experienced, are somehow threatened or undermined if
they can't be documented and explained to our families and
friends. If others don't know what we have gone through, if
they see us as the same people we were when we left (which
they invariably do), we feel cheated, as if our accomplishments
have somehow been diminished. The last words we want to hear
at the airport (and usually do) are: "You haven't changed a bit."
When we are already insecure about being homeless, it is not
encouraging to learn that our experiences may all have been for
nought.

We noted earlier that at least returnees don't have to adjust
to their own culture, that they know what to expect and how to
behave. At the same time, as the former expatriate knows well,
there's a difference between knowing what's going to happen
next and liking or approving of it. And this applies equally
overseas and at home. Indeed, to the extent sojourners adopt
and come to prefer certain behaviors of the foreign culture, the
home culture is no longer altogether their "own." There is,
then, some cultural adjustment called for during reentry, particularly of the kind described in chapter 5, where the individual
knows very well what to expect of the culture (harassment in
the cafe) but does not approve. In fact, there is even cultural
adjustment of the more fundamental sort, where the expatriate
must cope with behavior that's not expected, for after an extended sojourn abroad, the returnee comes to expect people everywhere to behave the way Ecuadorians or Kenyans do.

These are some of the challenges of reentry, some of the reasons why the return from abroad may not be the idyllic home-
coming we conjure up to comfort ourselves when the going gets
rough in Monrovia or Lahore. And the disappointment we feel
is all the more intense because this is, after all, our home,
where we expect to spend the rest of our lives. If we can't be
happy here, where *can* we be happy?

Fortunately, there are a number of steps newly returned sojourners can follow to take the sting out of reentry (steps we

picked up during our recent stint as foreigners). To begin with, being forewarned can take much of the shock out of the return. We might also remind ourselves that all transitions, whether from the familiar to the unfamiliar or, as in this case, vice versa, are inherently unsettling. And if we add to this the realization that what we are feeling is normal, that it is natural to find aspects of this experience unsettling, that there's nothing wrong with us—if we can remember these simple truths, we won't feel so anxious.

In this regard we should think back to our first few weeks abroad, when we faced many of these same problems and, as in the case of reentry, faced them all at once; we should recall that we managed to survive that experience and prosper. We have been through this before, in other words, and we can get through it again. But just as we were careful not to expect too much of ourselves at the beginning of our overseas sojourn, so we shouldn't expect too much immediately upon our arrival back home.

As for what steps to take, we would do well to apply the same technique of awareness we've been practicing abroad. We should realize we are reacting, appreciate the reason—because people are behaving in ways we are no longer used to—and refrain from judging and responding prematurely. The same advice applies to the phenomenon of resistance, when we try to hold on to behavior we picked up abroad and refuse to be absorbed back into our own culture: we should recognize that this is happening, understand why, and try to respond objectively.

REFERENCES

1. Bill Barich, *Traveling Light* (New York: Viking, 1984), ix.

2. V. S. Naipaul, *An Area of Darkness* (New York: Penguin, 1987), 43.

3. Francis Bacon, "Of Travel," in W. F. Williams, *A Book of English Essays* (New York: Penguin, 1980), 23.

4. Charles Allen, *Plain Tales From The Raj*, 260.

Afterword

So the journey is over and I am back again
where I started, richer by much experience and
poorer by many exploded convictions, many
perished certainties. For convictions and
certainties are too often the concomitants of
ignorance. Those who like to feel they are always
right and who attach a high importance to their
own opinions should stay at home. When one is
travelling, convictions are mislaid as easily as
spectacles; but unlike spectacles, they are not
easily replaced.

—ALDOUS HUXLEY
Jesting Pilate

We have seen in these pages that human beings, for all their
differences, share certain powerful beliefs and that among these
is the conviction that all other human beings are just like
them. In the main, this is good. In fact, it is more than good,
for this conviction sustains that element of predictability
that makes most human interaction possible. Yet there are circumstances, such as when people from two different cultures
meet, when that conviction does not apply and when the resulting interaction is awkward at best and may even break down
altogether.

Our purpose here has been to describe how this breakdown
comes about and to suggest a cure for it. To this end we have
presented a technique which permits individuals, with diligence
and discipline, to intervene in the cross-cultural process and
bend it to their will. And in this instance our wish is that we

should be able to learn enough about other people so that in due time we will come to expect them to be themselves.

This is an heroic goal, to escape for a moment the confines of the self. But it is not enough, as we have seen, that we should simply present a technique. Nor even that the reader should understand and accept it. The ease with which we grasp ideas has little bearing on whether we ever come to live by them. As we noted in chapter 4, a passing familiarity with the notion that it takes all kinds to make a world doesn't necessarily prepare us for the experience of meeting foreigners. So it is that a mere intellectual appreciation of the phenomenon of adjustment and the technqiue of awareness will not, by itself, produce any change in our behavior. We have to apply what we have understood—and apply it consistently over a sustained period—before we can expect results.

It would be wrong, meanwhile, to assume there is no urgency in this matter. The experience of living abroad profoundly transforms all who undergo it, whether they adjust to the culture or not. Such is the impact of the experience, at so many levels—physical, intellectual, emotional—there is not the possibility of a moderate, much less a neutral, reaction. We either open ourselves to the experience and are greatly enriched by it. Or we turn away and are greatly diminished.

APPENDIX

Americans

The trouble with other cultures is that the people don't behave the way they're supposed to, that is, like us. The solution to this difficulty is to stop expecting them to. And this we do by being aware of our erroneous expectations as they arise and by routing them. It isn't necessary, then, to understand exactly how we expect foreigners to be or what specific characteristics we expect them to exhibit.

Nevertheless, to have a sense of one's cultural self, of the qualities which comprise our distinctive national personality, can be a supporting factor in our progress toward true and last-ing adjustment. In this appendix we present a collection of ob-servations that have been made of Americans. In pinpointing how we are, they reveal how we expect others to be.

> I do envy these Europeans the comfort they take. When the work of the day is done, they forget it. Some of them go, with wife and children, to a beer hall and sit quietly and genteelly drinking a mug or two of ale and listening to music; others walk the streets, others drive in the avenues; others assemble in the great ornamental squares in the early evening to enjoy the sight and fragrance of flowers. . . . They go to bed moderately early and sleep well. They are always quiet, always orderly, always cheer-ful, comfortable and appreciative of life and its man-ifold blessings. The change that has come over our little party [of Americans] is surprising. Day by day we lose some of our restlessness and absorb some of

the spirit of quietude of the people. We grow wise
apace. We begin to comprehend what life is for.

—MARK TWAIN
The Innocents Abroad

Bold Talent shook his head. How like children
the Americans were, with their pranks and easy
warmth. Men who offered their hands for
strangers to shake, ladies who sat and chatted at
dinner with gentlemen they had never seen
before, children who threw snowballs at adults no
matter what their station. He would miss them.

—BETTY BAO LORD
Spring Moon

The people who are not pleased with America
must be those whose sympathies are fossilized or
whose eyes have no power of observation. Such
delightful and entertaining schemes for
hoodwinking nature you never saw, such
ingenuities for beating the terrible forces of the
seasons, such daring inventions and heroic tricks
of luxury. The people are bluff and good-natured
and as sharp as needles to detect and defy
pretension.

—EDMOND GOSSE
The Life and Letters of Sir Edmond Gosse

All Americans unsettled him; and most scared
him, either by their knowledge or their
ignorance, or both. But these two, blandly gazing
at him while he floundered for an answer,
inspired a spiritual alarm greater than anything
he was prepared for. They had too much energy,
even for Americans.

—JOHN LE CARRE
The Little Drummer Girl

All kinds of tourists are fair game for *touts*, but Americans seem their favorite targets, not just because of their careless ways with money and instinctive generosity, but also their non-European innocence about the viler dimensions of human nature and their desire to be liked, their impulse to say "Good morning" back instead of "Go away." It's a rare American who, asked "Where are you from sir?" will venture "Screw you" instead of "Boise."

—PAUL FUSSELL
Abroad

I'm not English. I'm American. We see all things as possible. We don't allow anyone to be better than ourselves.

—NORMAN MAILER
Manchester Guardian

An American? I looked up. "How do you know?" "Wearing a hat," he said. "Carrying her own boxes." "That doesn't mean she's an American." "Riding the night bus," he smiled. "American."

—PAUL THEROUX
The Consul's File

The best American travel writing, even today, is a more serious affair, usually because it is engaged upon a mission of national inquiry. It's not that Americans are innocents abroad or at home. It's just that they never quite know who they are or where they are at; therefore much of their travel writing is a strenuous effort to find out.

—ALEXANDER COCKBURN
"Bwana Vistas" *Harper's*, August 1984

Khoo Ah Au liked Americans. He found them, on the whole, generous, easygoing and completely predictable. They were rarely

ill-tempered as the British often were, or
eccentric in their demands, as were the French.
They did not harass him with questions he had
not been asked before and listened politely, if
sometimes inattentively, to the information he
had to impart. . . . Above all he found their
personal relationships easy to read. It was
probably a matter of race, he thought. His own
people were always very careful not to give
themselves away, to expose crude feelings about
one another. Americans seemed not to care how
much was understood by strangers. It was almost
as if they enjoyed being transparent.

—ERIC AMBLER
Passage of Arms

Americans have no capacity for abstract thought
and make bad coffee.

—GEORGES CLEMENCEAU

Here again was the American new world attitude
of bringing out the bulldozer to save someone
from an awful fate, or what America thought was
an awful fate. . . . I had not reckoned with the
naivete of Americans nor their lack of subtlety.

—LORD KILLANIN
My Olympic Years

If all things are transitory, let us find delight in
their transitoriness. We [in the West] welcome
change for its own sake and because of the joy we
take in it we have added a value to life. I think
it is America that has taught us this lesson, and
if that is so it is a greater benefit which that
country has conferred upon the world than

rag-time, cocktails, the phonograph and the
Pullman car.

—SOMERSET MAUGHAM
The Gentleman in the Parlor

Just in this one matter lies the charm of life in
Europe—comfort. In America we hurry, which is
well; but when the day's work is done, we go on
thinking of losses and gains, we plan for the
morrow, we even carry our business cares to béd
with us and toss and worry over them when we
ought to be restoring our racked bodies and
brains with sleep. We burn up our energies with
these excitements and either die early or drop
into a lean and mean old age at a time of life
which they call a man's prime in Europe. When
an acre of ground has produced long and well, we
let it lie fallow and rest for a season; we take no
man clear across the continent in the same
coach he started in—the coach is stabled
somewhere on the plains and its heated
machinery allowed to cool for a few days; when a
razor has seen long service and refuses to hold an
edge, the barber lays it away for a few weeks and
the edge comes back of its own accord. We
bestow thoughtful care upon inanimate objects
but none upon ourselves. What a robust people,
what a nation of thinkers we might be if we
would only lay ourselves on the shelves
occasionally to renew our edges.

—MARK TWAIN
The Innocents Abroad

I have always admired artlessness in others and
the Americans are fashioning a philosophy out of
it.

—PETER ACKROYD
The Last Testament of Oscar Wilde

Once we were out in a rural area in the middle of nowhere and saw an American come to a stop sign. Though he could see in both directions for miles and no traffic was coming, he still stopped!

—TURKISH EXCHANGE STUDENT IN
There Is a Difference

For me there was only one place to go if I couldn't live in my own country: America. It is a country of immigrants. There is such tolerance for the foreign and unfamiliar. America continues to amaze me.

—MILOS FORMAN
Time

Americans by and large have a hard time with abroad. Few tourists seem to have the patience to learn languages; fewer still can strike a balance between stubborn foreignness and overstrenuous attempts at integration—between the 10-gallon hat and the dhoti or kilt uncomfortably affected.

—DAVID ROBINSON
Times (London)

Civility cannot be purchased from Americans on any terms; they seem to think it is incompatible with freedom.

—ISAAC WELD

The biggest difference between ancient Rome and the USA is that in Rome the common man was treated like a dog. In America he sets the tone. This is the first country where the common man could stand erect.

—I. F. STONE

MacDonald's restaurants are probably a reflection
of our national character. They're fast . . .
they're efficient . . . they make money and
they're clean. If they're loud and crowded and if
the food is wastefully wrapped, packaged, boxed
and bagged . . . let's face it, Americans, that's
us.

—ANDY ROONEY
A Few Minutes with Andy Rooney

But as always happens, no matter how often one
visits America, the really overwhelming thing
was the affluence. . . . We should always
remember that when Americans talk about being
in a slump, they mean a slump by their
standards. For the visitor the sheer wealth of the
country must remain the abiding impression.

—CLIVE JAMES
Flying Visits

My book [*Brideshead Revisited*] has been a great
success in the United States which is upsetting
because I thought it in good taste before and now
I know it cannot be.

—EVELYN WAUGH
Letters of Evelyn Waugh

To escape from imposed systems, the yoke of
habit, family maxims, class prejudices, and to a
certain extent national prejudices as well: to treat
traditions as valuable for information only and to
accept existing facts as no more than a useful
sketch to show how things could be done
differently and better; to seek by themselves and
in themselves for the only reason for things,
looking for results without getting entangled in
the means toward them, and looking through
form to the basis of things—such are the

principal characteristics of what I would call the American philosophical method.

In a foreign land two Americans are friends at once for the simple reason that they are Americans. There is no prejudice to hold them back and their common fatherland draws them together. For two Englishmen the same blood is not enough; they must also have the same rank to bring them together.

Americans cleave to the things of this world as if assured that they will never die, and yet are in such a rush to snatch any that come within their reach, as if expecting to stop living before they have relished them. They clutch everything but hold nothing fast, and so lose grip as they hurry after some new delight. . . . An American will build a house in which to pass his old age and sell it before the roof is on. . . . He will take up one profession, and leave it, settle in one place and soon go off elsewhere. . . . At first sight there is something astonishing in this spectacle of so many lucky men restless in the midst of abundance. But it is a spectacle as old as the world; all that is new is to see a whole people performing it.

America is, I think, the only country on earth which has not taken the life of a single citizen for political offenses during the last fifty years.

—ALEXIS DE TOCQUEVILLE
Democracy in America

APPENDIX

A Selected Reading List

A number of well-known writers have commented on the matter of adaptation as is apparent from the quotes throughout this book. While adaptation is hardly ever their subject—the novelist is telling a story (which may feature expatriates) and the travel writer is relating a journey—these writers often reflect in passing on the experience of being foreign. And it is these asides we have made such frequent use of in these pages.

For the reader who might enjoy reading further, we offer the following list, a selection of works which contain more than the usual amount of cross-cultural observation and reflection. Even these books are not *about* adaptation, but their authors find the subject intriguing and return to it repeatedly.

GROWING
by Leonard Woolf

Woolf served for two years as a colonial administrator in Sri Lanka and came home and wrote a masterpiece. A young man, just discovering himself, Woolf puzzles over the meaning of his experiences and enlightens us all in the process. The prose is as rich as the observations it records.

JESTING PILATE
by Aldous Huxley

If Leonard Woolf hadn't written *Growing*, Huxley would get the nod as the master of reflective travel. In format, this is the standard narrative of a journey—from India throughout much of southeast Asia and the Pacific—but little happens that doesn't start Huxley thinking. And his thoughts lift this book clean out of its genre.

THE RAJ QUARTET
by Paul Scott

These four novels (*The Jewel in The Crown, The Towers of Silence, The Day of the Scorpion, A Division of the Spoils*) depict the British in India at the time of independence. The canvas is broad, but the theme is the meeting—and especially the clash—of two cultures. With the exception of Forster's *A Passage to India* (see below), these books come as close to being *about* crossing cultures as fiction can.

JOURNEY TO KARS
by Philip Glazebrook

Glazebrook, raised on stories of Victorian travelers to the Ottoman Empire, retraces their route and tries to understand the attraction. Why would these men leave the comforts of civilization at its apogee to wander the forbidding plains of Central Asia? In pursuing the answer, Glazebrook unravels the lure of abroad.

THE INNOCENTS ABROAD
by Mark Twain

Much of this book is standard travelogue, but enough of it is shrewd observation (usually in the form of hilarious satire) to secure it a place on our list. Twain marvels at what he sees (he travels throughout Europe and the Mediterranean), and we marvel at the transformation of his persona from the untutored Yank into the preening pseudo-sophisticate. Skip the guidebook descriptions of Italian cathedrals and watch for Twain's skewering of human nature.

A PASSAGE TO INDIA
by E. M. Forster

Adela Quested comes out from England to marry Ronny Heaslop and decides not to. The reason is India, or rather, how being in

India changes people. In exploring this subject (the same ground he covers in *A Room with a View*), Forster gets as close as any novelist ever has to the truth of the overseas experience.

THEIR HEADS ARE GREEN AND THEIR HANDS ARE BLUE
by Paul Bowles

A collection of essays set in Sri Lanka and North Africa, this book confirms that Bowles is as shrewd an observer of people and mores in nonfiction as he is in his excellent novels (*Let It Come Down*, *The Sheltering Sky*). As with the best travel writers, Bowles' experiences prompt him into reflection; he wants to understand. And we profit from listening in.

ESMOND IN INDIA
by Ruth Prawer Jhabvala

Esmond (from England) is beginning to regret his marriage to an upper-class Indian. Even more, he is bored with India. As he compares the Orient unflatteringly with the West and as Shakuntala struggles to understand her increasingly distant husband, we watch the chasm between cultures widen.

ABROAD
by Paul Fussell

This is a book about people who write travel books (it is subtitled *British Literary Travel between the Wars*). Fussell chronicles the careers of several of Britain's finest travel writers—Evelyn Waugh, D. H. Lawrence, Robert Byron—and examines how, through their books, England reached out to a wider world after the war to end all wars. *Abroad* is about the end of travel and the birth of tourism and how we are all poorer as a result.

THE LONG DAY WANES
(also known as *The Malayan Trilogy*)
by Anthony Burgess

These three novellas feature colonial expatriates in British Malaya before Malayan independence. The characters work hard to make sense out of the polyglot culture that surrounds them (part Indian, part Chinese, part Malay) and to understand their place—if any— therein.

PLAIN TALES FROM THE RAJ
by Charles Allen

Allen interviews the British who lived in—and ran—India prior to its independence. They describe their lives, and when they've finished, you know more than you might want to about expatriate subcultures.

THE CONSUL'S FILE
by Paul Theroux

An American runs a remote consulate in upcountry Malaysia. He's not very busy, which leaves him ample time to get involved in the life of the town and the affairs of the club. The consul is sufficiently jaded and sufficiently naive to make him a sharp, sympathetic observer.

THE LEFT HAND OF DARKNESS
by Ursula K. Le Guin
OUT OF THE SILENT PLANET
by C. S. Lewis

The action of most science fiction novels (such as these two) is triggered by the meeting of two different cultures (or "worlds" in the parlance). Le Guin and Lewis have written some of the classics of the genre. These two examples are virtual case studies of adaptation; while each has its own engaging story line, the subtext in both cases is the importance, if not the necessity, of understanding and adapting to the ways of an alien society.

Index

(including all authors quoted)